Polling and the public

Polling and the public

what every citizen should know

Herbert Asher
Ohio State University

A Division of Congressional Quarterly Inc.
1414 22nd Street N.W., Washington, D.C. 20037

Printed in the United States of America

Library of Congress Cataloging-in-Publication Data

Asher, Herbert B.
    Polling and the public: what every citizen should know / Herbert Asher.
       p.   cm.
    Bibliography: p.
    Includes index.
    ISBN 0-87187-402-4
    1. Public opinion polls. I. Title.
HM261.A74   1988   87-15339
303.3'8—dc 19   CIP

To my parents

Contents

Contents

Preface

Americans are no strangers to public opinion polls. Every week, pollsters sample their views on topics as diverse as presidential elections, mandatory blood testing for AIDS, and tax reform. The results of these polls influence discourse and decision making in every part of society and at the national, state, and local levels of government.

Despite their wide use, polls are not well understood. My central objective in writing this book, therefore, has been to help citizens become wiser consumers of public opinion polls. Because of the prevalence of public opinion polling, it is especially imperative that citizens be able to evaluate critically the various assertions made on the basis of the polls. Candidates for public office, incumbent officeholders, and many different public and private groups, for example, increasingly sponsor public opinion polls to advance their own objectives. Moreover, as polling data become more central to political discourse, an understanding of the factors that can influence poll results will enable citizens to participate more fully in that discourse.

Chapter 1 explains the types of polls, their importance, and the varying attitudes of citizens toward public opinion research. Chapters 2 through 5 address methodological aspects of polling such as the problem of nonattitudes, question wording and question order, sampling techniques, and interviewing procedures. These topics, while methodological in nature, are treated in a nontechnical fashion with numerous current examples and cartoons that illustrate important points. Chapters 6 through 8 are more analytical, focusing on how the media cover polls, the role of polls in elections and campaigns, and the interpretation of polls. The last chapter considers the role of polls in a democratic polity.

This book should be readily understandable to a diverse audience— college students taking courses in American politics, public opinion, communications, and journalism as well as practitioners in the fields of journalism and campaign management. In addition, the general public should find it helpful in evaluating the methods and merits of public opinion polls.

I am indebted to many people for their assistance in the preparation of this book. In particular, the reviewers of the manuscript—Paul Abramson and Doris Graber—provided many helpful comments and insights, as did Larry Baum, an Ohio State colleague. David Sweasey gave me invaluable help at all stages, and Barbara de Boinville was a very constructive and helpful copy editor. I would also like to thank Joanne Daniels, the director of CQ Press, for her encouragement, and Evamarie Socha for her diligence in expediting this book's production. The Department of Political Science and the Office of the President of The Ohio State University provided many useful resources.

Finally, I wish to express deep appreciation to the various polling organizations that are so generous in sharing their surveys with the broader public and that provided many of the substantive examples used herein. In particular, the CBS News/*New York Times* polls and the ABC News/*Washington Post* surveys have been an essential resource in the writing of this book, as have many of the newspaper articles written about these polls, particularly those by Barry Sussman and Adam Clymer.

Herbert Asher

Polling and the public

1

Americans today are bombarded with the results of public opinion polls sponsored by the major news media, candidates for public office, incumbent officeholders, and many different public and private organizations. These polls are increasingly used not only to inform citizens about what their compatriots believe, but also to convince and even manipulate them in ways advantageous to the polls' sponsors. The aim of this book is to help citizens become more astute judges of the polls so that they will not be misled and deceived by assertions made on the basis of polling data. This will be accomplished by explaining in nontechnical language the various factors that can affect poll results, such as question wording, sampling, and interviewing, and by critiquing various types and uses of polls.

The importance of polls

But why should citizens become more astute consumers of the polls? There are other more positive reasons than simply to avoid being manipulated by those who use the polls inappropriately to promote their own ends. For some individuals, public opinion polling will be the basis on which they make major economic and career decisions. For example, the businessperson who commissions a survey on customer preferences or the television station manager who underwrites a survey on audience demographics will use the obtained information to make important decisions. Likewise, the potential candidate for public office may commission a poll to assess his or her electoral prospects prior to deciding whether to run. In these examples the polling is likely to be conducted by a commercial polling organization. But if the businessperson and the would-be candidate are knowledgeable about polls, they will be better able to communicate their objectives and requirements for the poll to the survey organization and to apply the results of the survey to their own decision making.

Polls are important for the average citizen as well as the business-person and potential candidate. The polls today have become a major way in which Americans learn what their fellow citizens are thinking. The substantial media coverage of polls provides citizens with the opportunity to compare their own beliefs with their compatriots' and to learn whether their own views are shared by others. As citizens use the polls in this manner, they need to be aware of the factors that affect the poll results so that they do not accept or reject them too quickly.

Polling has become an integral part of political events at the national, state, and local levels. There is seldom a major event or decision in which poll results are not a part of the news media's coverage and the decision makers' deliberations. How should an international crisis be resolved? Should state taxes be raised? What is the best location for a new library in the community? Polls help politicians make these kinds of decisions, and in order for citizens to follow all aspects of the polls, a knowledge of the essentials of public opinion polling is required.

Finally, the role of public opinion polls in political discourse in the United States is likely to increase due to the improved technology of polling, the introduction of courses in polling methodology in journalism curricula, the widespread assumption (challenged by Benjamin Ginsberg in Chapter 9) that polls are the best way to measure public opinion, and the belief that public opinion polls are instruments of democracy since they allow everyone's views to be represented. All of these factors ensure that future political debate on issues will be characterized by even greater reliance on the polls. To participate in this political debate in an informed and analytical fashion, Americans will have to come to grips with the public opinion polls—a useful tool of government and a valuable source of information to citizens and leaders alike.

The pervasiveness of polls

That public opinion polling has become a growth industry in the United States is undeniable. The polls most familiar to Americans are those conducted for and reported by the major communications media. For

2

example, each of the three major television networks sponsors polls in collaboration with a print medium—CBS News with the *New York Times*, ABC News with the *Washington Post*, and NBC News with the *Wall Street Journal*. Likewise, the major news magazines often commission polls on national issues; thus, *Newsweek* regularly employs the Gallup Organization, Inc., while *Time* utilizes Yankelovich Clancy Shulman.

Typically, these polls survey citizens about their views on the issues, candidates, and incumbents (especially the president); their preferences about possible courses of governmental action; and their general attitudes toward politics and the political process. Major national polls also regularly cover tax reform, social values, hostage crises, abortion, foreign policy, the budget deficit, and countless other political and nonpolitical topics.

Sometimes survey questions seem to violate standards of good taste. After President Ronald Reagan's surgery for what turned out to be cancer of the colon, a survey commissioned by *Time* asked respondents how serious they thought the president's health problems were and whether he was likely to serve his full term. An ABC News/*Washington Post* poll asked Americans whether the president was likely to complete his term. And a *Newsweek* poll inquired whether citizens were concerned that the president might not "be able to meet the demands of a second term." Many citizens undoubtedly had questions in their own minds about the president's health, and therefore the media thought it would be interesting to their readers and viewers to ask questions on the matter—hence the ghoulish speculation. Indeed, when an issue or event becomes visible and especially controversial, the public is usually surveyed to assess its reaction. Thus, when Bernard Goetz in 1984 shot four youths who had accosted him on a New York subway, it provided a dramatic and salient topic on which to survey a public that was very aware of the incident. Likewise, as the acquired immune deficiency syndrome (AIDS) received renewed publicity in the summer of 1985 and became the cover story in both *Time* and *Newsweek*, Americans were polled about their own attitudes and fears about the disease and what the government should do. All of these examples illustrate that poll results about newsworthy stories often become a part of the stories themselves.

Just as there are prominent national polls, so are there visible and reputable state and local polls focusing often on specific state and local matters and on national affairs as well. For example, the *Daily News* (New York) and Eyewitness News (the ABC-TV affiliate in New York City) have polled New Yorkers about their views concerning the New

3

York police, Mayor Ed Koch, the firing of Yogi Berra as manager of the Yankees and his replacement by Billy Martin, the likelihood of the Yankees and Mets making the World Series, and other matters of local concern. Likewise, the *New York Times* in conjunction with WCBS-TV did an extensive study of race relations in New York City. In many states there are first-rate polling organizations, often affiliated with a university and/or a major news medium. For example, the Eagleton Institute at Rutgers University working with the *Newark Star-Ledger* surveys New Jerseyans about their state and its government and about New Jersey as a place to live. Finally, publications such as *Public Opinion Quarterly* provide summaries of various poll results.

The polls described thus far are certainly the most prominent and probably the most credible to the American public. Their prominence comes from the often substantial media coverage their results receive; their credibility derives from the public's perception that they are scientific and that the media and other entities that sponsor the polls are themselves legitimate and objective. The factor most critical in making these polls scientific (and useful) is the careful selection of a sample of respondents (most often 1,000 to 1,500 persons), which enables one to generalize from the sample to the population from which the sample was drawn. It is impossible to interview directly the entire adult American population of 160 million; a representative sample of 1,500 respondents who have been properly interviewed makes possible (within certain limits to be discussed later) appropriate statements about the overall population.

Commissioned polls _____

Polls by the major news media represent only the tiniest fraction of the public opinion polling that is being done in the United States. Many other organizations conduct polls, many of them of high quality, others of lesser repute. Polls are conducted for purposes other than informing citizens. Many clients and companies have questions they need answered and therefore commission polls; many academic investigators have research questions that require the use of surveys. The results of these polls may not receive great public attention, but they still can have an effect on individual citizens.

An excellent example of a commissioned poll is one paid for by the Internal Revenue Service (IRS) in 1984 to study the problem of tax cheating. Among the items in the survey were these statements to which the respondent was supposed to agree or disagree:

It's not so wrong to hold back a little bit on taxes since the government spends too much anyway.

The present tax system benefits the rich and is unfair to the ordinary working man or woman.

Since a lot of rich people pay no taxes at all, if someone like me underpays a little, it's no big deal. (Sussman 1984c, 36.)

The study found that 19 percent of the respondents admitted cheating on their returns; young, upwardly mobile professionals were the most likely to cheat. The study also investigated ways to reduce cheating and found that Americans strongly rejected the use of paid informants to catch cheaters (Sussman 1985c). Although the honesty of tax cheaters' responses to questions about tax cheating is questionable, the IRS probably gained some useful insights about the magnitude of the cheating problem and the feasibility of alternative solutions.

This IRS study is typical of thousands of studies that have been commissioned by public and private bodies to address specific concerns. Some of these surveys are based on national samples; others are based on specialized samples that are more appropriate to the research questions being addressed. For example, the *Washington Post* in 1985 conducted a telephone survey of university presidents' views on the state of intercollegiate athletics. A recent promotional brochure of the Gallup Social Science Research Group, a division of the Gallup Organization, listed some of the social research surveys it had conducted. These included:

American College of Surgeons. A national personal interview survey of the general public and members of Congress to measure opinions related to surgeons and surgical care.

New Jersey State Lottery Commission. A marketing survey using telephone interviews to ... aid policymakers in reaching decisions regarding future growth of the New Jersey State Lottery.

Federal Energy Administration. A series of personal interview surveys on attitudes toward and use of home insulation.

Catholic Press Association. A television survey of readers of local diocesan newspapers and religious magazines on attitudes toward religious media.

American Jewish Committee. Semi-annual surveys of the national general public on attitudes related to Israel.

Japan Embassy. An annual national personal interview survey of the general public and mail survey of opinion leaders on attitudes toward Japan.

Commissioned surveys of this type are likely to be high-quality enterprises mainly because the sponsors have a genuine need for accurate information to address some organizational goal or problem. To that end, the sponsors employ a reputable outfit, such as the Gallup Organization or Louis Harris and Associates, to design and conduct the survey and perhaps to analyze the data and interpret the results as well. Many other groups, however, do surveys for a different reason—not to address scientifically and objectively a public concern, but instead to promote a certain position and to convince the public of the wisdom of it. To that end the survey will be designed to yield the desired results; this is most often accomplished by the use of highly loaded questions, although more subtle methods are also used. Sometimes the samples interviewed are skewed to ensure a predetermined outcome. In many cases the poll itself is secondary to the real aim of the group—namely, to raise money to support its objectives.

With the advent of computerized mailings, many organizations have entered the direct mail fund-raising and polling business. In fact, most often the polling becomes a device to generate donations as the sponsoring organization encourages recipients of the mailings to make their views known *and* to contribute to a good cause. Many of these appeals come from political groups, some broad in scope, such as the Democratic and Republican parties, and others more narrow in focus, such as the Wilderness Society, the Union of Concerned Scientists, the National Right to Work Committee, the Religious Coalition for Abortion Rights, and many, many others.

For example, the Republican National Committee in 1981 mailed a National Legislative Action Survey to thousands of potential contributors on the GOP's mailing lists. The survey included nine questions as well as a direct appeal for funds. The use of the poll to generate donations is illustrated by the text of the mailing (see box, above opposite). The Democrats have lagged behind the GOP in the use of computerized mailings, but the 1985 Economic and National Issues Survey sponsored by the Democratic Senatorial Campaign Committee demonstrates that they too have learned how advantageous it is to attach a poll to a fund-raising effort (see box, below opposite).

Concerned groups and individuals have used the newspapers to promote their views and conduct polls. On March 7, 1983, the Moral Majority took out a full-page advertisement in the *Washington Post* on the nuclear freeze. At the bottom of the advertisement was a three-item questionnaire that readers were encouraged to complete and return to the Reverend Jerry Falwell, who in turn would report the results to our

TO: **Richard Richards, Chairman**

FROM: **Herb Asher**

I strongly support President Reagan's program to limit federal spending, cut my taxes, bring down inflation and rebuild our national defense. And I agree he needs my support to offset the power of the special interest groups operating on Capitol Hill.

I have filled out the National Legislative Action Survey. You have my permission to tabulate, record and release my responses as part of the total national Survey results.

Please inform the press, the Congress, Republican Party leaders and candidates of the final Survey results since I believe it will give dramatic, tangible proof that Americans support President Reagan's policies.

Please use my contribution to 1) mail the National Legislative Action Survey to more Americans and 2) fund our campaign to elect a Republican majority to Congress and the state legislatures in 1982 to assure President Reagan's programs are not overturned.

☐ $15   ☐ $25   ☐ $50   ☐ $100   ☐ $250   ☐ $500   ☐ $_____ other

I've made my check payable to: Republican National Committee

national leaders. One of the questions was, "Are you willing to trust the survival of America to a nuclear freeze agreement with the Soviet Union, a nation which rejects on-site inspection of military facilities to insure compliance?" In case the question wording itself was not sufficiently loaded to generate a negative response, the text of the advertisement warned of the Soviet threat.

Indeed, many groups mail highly one-sided literature and then ask the respondent for his or her opinion. Consider these examples. The Committee Against Government Waste asked, "Before you received this letter, were you aware of the gross mismanagement and waste of funds

DSCC RESPONSE FORM

I REALIZE THAT ideas are critically important to the future of our Party and our country. So I've filled out my Economic and National Issues Survey and am returning it to you. Please make certain the findings of this survey are known to each Democratic senator.

ALSO . . . I'm determined to help restore the Senate of the United States to Democratic Party control. So I've enclosed a contribution to help the *Democratic Senatorial Campaign Committee* build a strong financial base for the 1986 elections. My check is enclosed for:

☐ $20   ☐ $25   ☐ $35   ☐ $50   ☐ $75   ☐ $100   ☐ Other $_____

Dr Herbert B Asher

Please make your check payable to the DSCC and return it with this form and your survey in the enclosed postage paid envelope to: P.O. Box 37260, Washington, D.C. 20013.

A132   124255

in the U.S. Department of Defense's purchase of parts?" The American Farmland Trust asked, "Were you aware of the gravity of the problem of our vanishing farmland before receiving this mailing?" In case the literature accompanying the poll does not convince the respondent of the correctness of the group's position, a carefully constructed question or statement may achieve the same end as illustrated by the following items and sponsoring organizations:

> Are you in favor of allowing construction union czars the power to shut down an entire construction site because of a dispute with a single contractor, thus forcing even more workers to knuckle under to union agents? *National Right to Work Committee*

> In his speeches and public addresses, the President has always made a point of keeping the American people fully informed of the Soviet threat to world peace. The Democrats, on the other hand, constantly downplay the Soviet threat. Do you think that, during his campaign, the President should continue to bring this issue to the attention of the voters?
> ___ Yes, the President should continue to address the Soviet threat
> ___ No, I agree with the Democrats who downplay the Soviet threat
> ___ Not sure *Republican National Committee*

> Were you aware that a good part of why America has been leaning toward nuclear weapons is due to inflated prices of conventional weapons parts? *Committee Against Government Waste*

> The Reagan Administration must replace the James Watt political appointees who have been carrying out destructive land policies and will continue to do so until they're removed. *The Wilderness Society*

> Teenagers, through the force of law and regardless of circumstance such as rape and incest, should be denied access to abortion services until their parents are notified, or until they have obtained a court order. *Religious Coalition for Abortion Rights*

> Do you endorse the idea that a greater number of smaller farms should be encouraged to relieve the growing burden being placed on large farms to fulfill our agricultural needs? *American Farmland Trust*

> Our nation is still blessed with millions of acres of public lands, including roadless wilderness areas, forests and range lands. Land developers, loggers, and mining and oil companies want to increase their operations on these public lands. Do you think these remaining pristine areas of your public lands should be protected from such exploitation? *Sierra Club*

All of the preceding items were constructed to generate responses sympathetic to the sponsors' objectives. In fact, some readers might object on a number of grounds to even calling these enterprises *polling*.

First, in most cases there is no scientifically selected sample; instead the surveys and fund-raising requests are mailed out to lists of citizens who are thought to be likely supporters. There is little concern about whether the people who actually respond are in some way representative of a larger population. Second, the questions are often poorly formulated and fundamentally flawed (deliberately so). Third, in many cases the survey data collected may never be tabulated; if tabulated, little analysis can be conducted since the original survey was very short and omitted key questions about the demographic and political characteristics of the respondents.

Orton (1982) has identified other examples of what he calls *pseudo polls*. The representativeness of the respondents to these polls is highly questionable. For example, the print and electronic media often encourage their audience to write or phone to express their views. But even with hundreds or thousands of replies, these straw polls are usually unrepresentative simply because people who would voluntarily choose to participate are likely to differ in important ways from the overall population. They may be more interested, informed, and concerned about the topic at hand and thus hold views different from those of the overall population. A prominent example of a pseudo poll occurred in 1980 when ABC News encouraged viewers to call (at a cost of fifty cents) to indicate whether they thought Jimmy Carter or Ronald Reagan had won the presidential debate.

Other examples of pseudo polls are the questionnaires that representatives distribute to households within their congressional districts. Typically, these are addressed to "postal customer," and there is no sure way of knowing just who in the household actually completed the survey. Although thousands of these questionnaires may be returned to a congressional office, it is very difficult to ascertain whether the respondents' demographic characteristics and actual opinions on the issues are truly representative of the broader constituency. In some instances the questions themselves are loaded to guarantee responses compatible with the member of Congress's own predisposition and record. This is not to say that the completed questionnaires are ignored or discarded; in most cases the results are tabulated and later reported to the constituency in a newsletter. But, as Sussman (1985h, 37) argues, these questionnaires are mainly "a public relations gimmick, aimed at convincing voters that officeholders care about the folks back home."

Despite their deficiencies, I prefer to include these unscientific enterprises and the more scientific surveys discussed earlier together under the rubric of polling. Citizens are subjected to many different kinds of polls, all of which may affect them in some way. Hence, it becomes important for citizens to be aware of the gamut of polls and to be able to evaluate them appropriately. If citizens are able to recognize unscientific polls and their associated deficiencies (as well as the shortcomings of scientific polls), then they are less likely to be misled by the results of such surveys. This leads us to the central concern of this book—the citizen as a potential consumer of public opinion polls.

The citizen as a consumer of polls

As argued earlier in this chapter, opinion polling is pervasive in the United States. Whatever the quality of these polls, they all can affect the attitudes and behavior of citizens. Even those media-sponsored polls designed to inform the audience (and perhaps to keep up with the competition and improve ratings) may do more than simply report citizens' attitudes. They may also help shape preferences, particularly during the presidential primary season when polling is frequent and the linkages between a candidate's poll standing, media coverage, and primary election fate are pronounced. (The role of polls in elections will be considered in Chapter 7.)

There are highly specific polls designed to affect behavior; for example, it has become increasingly common to use public opinion surveys in court proceedings dealing with change of venue motions (Nietzel and Dillehay 1983) and in cases concerning protection of trademarks and advertising claims (Dutka 1982). Public opinion research has been conducted on almost any topic imaginable, whether it be opinions on midwifery and home birth (DeClerq 1983), computers (Morrison 1983), artificial insemination (Reading, Sledmere and Cox 1982), death and funerals (Marks and Calder 1982), animal-based research (Grodsky 1983), the rights of mental patients (Brown 1982), male attitudes toward menopause (Neevel 1982), or forensic psychiatry (Slater and Hans 1984).

Americans are major consumers of the results of public opinion research. But are they smart consumers? Americans should be aware of the problems and limitations of polls before they "buy" anything from them. Just as the customer in a supermarket will often inspect the list of ingredients in a product, so should the public opinion consumer question what went into the poll before accepting its results. This is particularly important because in many instances the citizen is not simply a passive consumer of polls. Instead, there is often someone who is actively promoting the poll results to generate support for his or her objectives. It might be the president utilizing polls to argue that the American people support his policies. It might be a local builder with a neighborhood poll purporting to show local support for a rezoning ordinance to permit commercial construction in an area. It might be a regional transportation commission citing poll results to justify the establishment of bus lanes on freeways. Or it might be a friend or neighbor selectively using poll results to win an argument with you.

Citizens should become better consumers of public opinion research, but they need not become experts at drawing samples, constructing questionnaires, and analyzing data. An intuitive awareness of the steps involved in a survey and the possible consequences of these steps will make the consumer of polls better able to reject bad merchandise and to appreciate good buys. Thus, the major aim of this book is to sensitize citizens to the problems and limitations of opinion polling. This book should in no way be construed as a condemnation of public opinion research; most of the highly publicized polls as well as the private polls reflect the highest standards of polling. But there is an art to the conduct and analysis of surveys. An appreciation of that art will leave the citizen less susceptible to the tyranny that may occur when a public opinion poll is deemed by its sponsor to be scientific and its results therefore unchallengable.

A number of methodological points will be raised in this book, often in the context of important substantive examples. Chapter 2 addresses the problem of nonattitudes. Sometimes the topic of a poll is inappropriate; that is, citizens do not have genuine attitudes on the topic and yet they still answer the questions. This is the problem of nonattitudes; despite pollsters' best efforts, citizens will often respond to questions on which they have no real opinions, thereby yielding a misleading portrait of public opinion.

Chapter 3 discusses question wording and question order and context. Numerous examples of poorly worded questions likely to produce skewed results have already been cited. But not only is the wording of individual questions important. A survey is a series of questions, and the placement and context of those questions can greatly affect the obtained results.

Chapter 4 focuses on various sampling techniques and their advantages and disadvantages. It also deals with sample size and sampling error. Like sampling techniques, interviewing techniques are extremely important. Chapter 5 explains in detail how different interviewing procedures can affect the results.

BLOOM COUNTY   **by Berke Breathed**

© 1983, Washington Post Writers Group, reprinted with permission.

Chapter 6 examines how the media report the polls, and Chapter 7 analyzes the role of polls in elections. Since Americans learn about the polls primarily through the mass media, how the media report polls greatly influences public opinion. This is particularly interesting in the case of high-visibility national polls because the medium that reports the polls also has responsibility for conducting them. Chapter 7 argues that the polls have come to play an intrusive role in elections and that the use of polls by candidates and the reporting of polls by the media often do a disservice to the citizen and to the electoral process. Elections are the most visible opportunity for citizens to influence their government, and to the extent that polls affect that opportunity, citizens should be sensitive to the role of polls in elections. As Chapter 8 explains, the analysis of poll results is more of an art than a science with many opportunities for the manipulative interpretation and dissemination of poll results in order to sway public opinion. The last chapter ties together the various themes, offers suggestions about better utilization of polls, and discusses the effects of the polls on the American polity.

Before turning to Chapter 2 and the problem of nonattitudes, two tasks remain to be done in this chapter. The first is to consider the confidence of citizens in the polls. If one is concerned about the citizen as consumer, one first needs to know how the citizen feels about the polls. Certainly, a citizenry skeptical and suspicious of the polls is much less likely to be manipulated by them. The chapter will then conclude with a discussion of the role of polling in a democratic polity. Advocates and critics of the polls have long argued whether the polls contribute to or undermine the workings of our democratic society.

Citizens' views of the polls _____

Reactions to public opinion polling by ordinary citizens are generally positive, although there are specific areas of criticism and skepticism. Among political elites the view of polls is often more critical. In 1985 the Gallup and Roper organizations both conducted national surveys that assessed popular awareness of and reactions to the public opinion polls (Clymer 1985; Sussman 1985e). Twenty-five percent of the respondents in the Gallup survey said that they regularly followed the results of a public opinion poll in a newspaper or magazine; an additional 16 percent did so occasionally. Fifty-nine percent of the respondents said that they did not follow a poll regularly in the print medium; of course, they might sporadically be attentive to polls in print, or they might be aware of the polls through the electronic media, particularly television.

With respect to the accuracy of the polls, both the Gallup and Roper surveys indicated fairly positive views by Americans. More than two-thirds of the Gallup sample said the polls were right most of the time, while 56 percent of the respondents to the Roper survey said the polls were almost always or usually accurate. Likewise, the media, the sponsors of the most widely reported polls, are generally given high marks for being accurate and fair, although public confidence in television and newspapers is lower today than in the 1970s, according to an October 22, 1984, *Newsweek* poll. Finally, 76 percent of the persons in the Gallup survey thought that polls were a good thing in our country, and only 12 percent thought they were a bad thing.

Despite these indications of positive attitudes toward the polls, other evidence, often of an anecdotal nature, suggests a more skeptical view by the public. Most teachers and practitioners of public opinion polling have encountered citizens who have expressed utter disbelief in polling. Some citizens complain that they and their friends and relatives have never been interviewed and therefore wonder just how representative samples can be. This kind of skepticism is widespread. Koch (1985) found that persons who had never participated in a poll were dubious about the accuracy of the results of surveys.

Others' doubts arise from the size of the samples selected. In talking about polling with diverse audiences, I repeatedly hear people ask how a sample of 1,500 respondents can possibly represent 160 million adult Americans. And despite my brilliant answer by analogy—a doctor takes only a sample of a person's blood (fortunately) and a chef need taste only a spoonful of soup (assuming the soup is stirred properly) to test its seasoning—much skepticism about the polls remains. Indeed, one

13

DON'T FORGET THAT ELECTION YEAR IS
ALSO LIE-TO-THE-POLLSTERS YEAR.

question posed in the 1985 Roper survey showed that only 28 percent of
Americans believed that national polls with sample sizes of 1,500 to
2,000 could be accurate, while 56 percent said they could not be
(Sussman 1985e).

One substantive area in which the polls have received much
criticism is their growing role in elections and election coverage by the
media. The argument is often made that polls have contributed to the
packaging of candidates; aspiring leaders are accused of first consulting
the polls and then staking out their positions, thereby abdicating their

leadership responsibilities on issues. Similarly, the use of polls in reporting elections is seen as encouraging a horse-race mentality among the media; instead of focusing on issues and the candidates' qualifications, the dominant theme becomes who's ahead and who's behind, who's gaining and who's falling back, as measured by the polls.

Exit polls, interviews with citizens right after they have finished voting, enable the networks to project election outcomes even before the polls are closed. This practice has angered many citizens and political elites. Columnist Mike Royko has encouraged voters to lie to exit pollsters. Congress has conducted hearings in an effort to get the networks to alter voluntarily the ways in which they report exit polls and election projections. Other observers have condemned the impact of polls on American politics, none more harshly than Daniel Greenberg who wrote:

> Given the devastation that opinion surveys have brought to the American political process, we shouldn't be asking how polls can be sharpened but rather why they are endured and how they can be banished.
>
> Polls are the life-support system for the finger-to-the-wind, quick-change politics of our time and, as such, are the indispensable tools for the ideologically hollow men who work politics like a soap-marketing campaign....
>
> The effect of this—on campaigns, as well as on administrations between campaigns—is an obsession with salesmanship rather than with governance.... (Greenberg 1980, A-17)

The nation's political cartoonists, many of whom are syndicated in newspapers that themselves conduct polls, have had a field day attacking the polls, particularly their frequency, duration, and intrusiveness in the presidential selection process.

Although sometimes angry or skeptical about poll results, Americans generally think they are accurate and fair. Americans often resent the intrusiveness and presumed power of the polls, yet they eagerly consume the latest public opinion findings about a myriad of topics. This schizoid love-hate relationship is probably inevitable in our political system. We all want our voices to be heard and therefore attack the polls when it appears that they are undermining genuine citizen involvement and influence. Yet in a large and heterogeneous nation such as the United States, the polls may be the best mechanism for reflecting the diversity of public opinion. The very simple fact that polls generally count all respondents equally bestows upon polls a democratic character that enhances their appeal in a democratic society.

15

Polling and democracy _____

The role of polling in a democratic society has been a controversial one. Advocates of polling point to the participation of the citizenry in a democracy and praise the polls since they permit the quick and repeated assessment of the opinions of the public. Polling is particularly valued by those who prefer a direct democracy in which the people govern directly rather than through intermediaries such as elected representatives. There is a fascination today with the possibility that technological innovations such as the development of interactive cable television might facilitate direct governance by the citizenry. Until its recent demise, the QUBE system in Columbus, Ohio, was seen as the wave of the future; Columbus residents on the QUBE system were able to vote from their homes on issues of the day and have their choices tabulated instantly. Indeed, NBC News used the QUBE facilities to conduct an instant survey of viewers' reactions to President Carter's 1979 speech in which he said that reducing America's dependence on foreign oil was the moral equivalent of war.

Some proponents of a more traditional, representative notion of democratic theory also welcome the public opinion polls because they provide systematic information on the preferences of the citizenry. It is argued that citizens' opinions should influence the behavior of their elected representatives and that any mechanism such as polls that provide information on citizens' opinions is bound to foster democracy. Obviously, there is mixed empirical evidence about the extent to which popular preferences are actually translated into public policy. We can all cite examples of the government's seeming unresponsiveness to public opinion. Polls regularly show that overwhelming majorities of Americans favor some form of gun control such as handgun registration, yet Congress has never passed such a measure and in 1986 actually voted to weaken existing firearms legislation. However, a number of empirical studies (Page and Shapiro 1983; Erikson 1976) have found substantial congruence between the attitudes of the public and the actions of government. And while these studies are careful not to attribute too quickly government decisions to popular preferences, they do suggest conditions under which citizen influence is likely to be significant.

Other observers worry about the harmful consequences of polls for a democratic political system. They agree that citizen influence is a key component of a democracy and that, properly measured, public opinion can be useful in governing. But they argue that polls give a misleading impression of how a democracy actually operates. Public opinion is not

16

synonymous with the results of public opinion polls, yet today the two are treated as if they were identical. A focus solely on poll results ignores the dynamics of opinion formation and change and often overlooks factors that may shape (and manipulate) public opinion such as leadership and interest group behavior. Polls present an overall portrait of the distribution of opinion, but their reporting and use often ignore important differences in preferences among subgroups, thereby yielding a misleading picture of attitudinal similarity across different segments of the American population. Margolis (1984) claims that polls may not be the optimal way to measure public opinion on politically and socially sensitive topics. Actual behavior in some instances provides a more valid expression of public opinion, he asserts, than do verbal responses to survey questions.

A more radical criticism of the polls is that they are simply a sop to the citizenry, that they give people a false sense of being influential when in reality political power is held and exercised by a few elites who may or may not act in the public's interest. Social scientist Johan Galtung (1969) made the point most effectively when he argued that surveys are too democratic: they generally count all respondents equally, whereas there are tremendous disparities among people in the resources and skills they bring to bear on political decisions. To the extent that a survey is seen as a quasi referendum on issues, it is misleading since the participants in the referendum have differential opportunities to shape governmental outcomes.

Another major criticism of the polls is their consequences for leadership in the United States. The simplistic version of this criticism is that leaders blindly follow the polls rather than work to educate and persuade the public. Others argue that leaders have been weakened by the polls because the widespread awareness of public preferences generated by the polls limits the ability of leaders to make unpopular choices. Others complain that leaders can easily manipulate the polls (perhaps by giving a major televised address) and therefore generate poll results unfairly supportive of their policies. A more fundamental point is made that polls (and the media) have altered the style and substance of governance, particularly by emphasizing immediate consequences and the next election. The result is a short-sighted approach to problem solving, they claim. In defense of the polls' impact on leadership, it is argued that officials should have information about citizens' attitudes prior to making decisions and that the polls, whatever their limitations, are the best way to acquire that information.

What then do we conclude about opinion polls in the United States?

"Bring me my pipe, my bowl, my fiddlers three, and my pollster."

Obviously, they are now an integral part of our political and social landscape, and they are likely to become even more prominent in the future. Polls can provide useful information to citizens and leaders; they also can be highly misleading and inaccurate. Polls may enhance the opportunities for citizen influence; they can also serve to manipulate the public. The late George Gallup wrote optimistically about the future of the polls:

> As students, scholars, and the general public gain a better understanding of polls, they will have a greater appreciation of the service polls can perform in a democracy. In my opinion, modern polls are the chief hope of lifting government to a higher level, by showing that the public supports the reforms that will make this possible, by providing a *modus operandi* for testing new ideas. . . . Polls can help make govern-

ment more efficient and responsive; they can improve the quality of candidates for public office; they can make this a truer democracy. (Gallup 1965-1966, 549)

More than two decades have passed since these claims were made, and current discourse about the polls has become much more critical. Nevertheless, to the extent that citizens become wiser consumers of the polls, to that extent will Gallup's lofty aspirations for the polls be realized.

The problem of nonattitudes 2

To produce an informative and accurate public opinion poll, a number of tasks must be successfully performed. A questionnaire with properly worded and ordered questions must be constructed. A representative sample must be selected and the respondents in that sample correctly interviewed. The data must be analyzed appropriately and the correct conclusions drawn. But before any of these tasks can be performed, a fundamental question must be asked: Is the proposed topic of the poll one on which citizens have genuine opinions? If it is, then the topic is suitable for a public opinion survey. But if the topic is so remote and irrelevant to citizens' concerns that they do not possess real views on it, then a poll on the topic will measure *nonattitudes* rather than attitudes. Any information obtained will be suspect even though the questions are properly worded, the sample scientifically selected, and the data appropriately analyzed.

The problem of nonattitudes is one of the simplest yet most complex problems in public opinion polling. Too often in the survey context people will respond to questions about which they have no genuine attitudes or opinions.[1] Even worse, these nonattitude responses are treated by the analyst as if they represented actual public opinions. Hence, a misleading portrait of public opinion may emerge if a distinction is not made between people with real views on an issue and those whose responses simply reflect their desire to appear to be informed citizens in the interview situation. Unfortunately, it is often very difficult to differentiate between genuine attitude holders and persons merely expressing nonattitudes.

The presence of nonattitudes in survey responses has been well documented (Converse 1970; Taylor 1983; Norpoth and Lodge 1985). A particularly intriguing study was carried out by Bishop, Oldendick, and

21

Tuchfarber (1980) in which a fictitious item was included in surveys conducted in the greater Cincinnati area. Respondents were presented with the following item about the nonexistent Public Affairs Act: "Some people say that the 1975 Public Affairs Act should be repealed. Do you agree or disagree with this idea?" Fully a third of the respondents offered an opinion on this version of the question. When an effort was made to filter out nonattitude responses on this fictitious question, 10 percent of the sample still offered an opinion. (The use of screening or filter questions will be discussed later in this chapter.) Nonattitudes are definitely a problem for would-be interpreters of public opinion.

The existence of nonattitudes is not surprising; after all, the interview is a social situation in which the respondent interacts in person or over the phone with an interviewer whom the respondent does not know. Few in such a circumstance want to admit that they are uninformed, particularly on an issue about which they might be expected by others to be informed. Most people answer the questions, and their responses are duly recorded by the interviewer. Before discussing ways to address the problem of nonattitudes, I would like to illustrate how a public opinion survey based on nonattitudes can go astray and mislead the public.

An example of nonattitudes

About ten years ago I was part of a sample of Ohioans queried about their views on land use problems. The interview was conducted over the phone, and the sample was probably picked from the telephone book. (I surmised this since the interviewer knew my name.) After the interviewer identified herself and the sponsorship of the poll, she asked:

> Tell me, Mr. Asher, what comes to your mind when you hear the term *land use?*

As a social scientist familiar with public opinion polling, I recognized this question to be a screening question to determine whether it was worthwhile for the interviewer to proceed with the interview with me. Surely, if I did not have the vaguest idea what land use meant, there would be little point in continuing the interview. In any event I responded to the interviewer:

> Hmmm. Land use. How you use the land!

This response must have been sufficiently brilliant for the interviewer continued with the survey. She asked me:

Mr. Asher, what do you think is the most important land use problem facing Ohio?

I mentally squirmed and silently gave thanks that I was not wired up to electrodes for they would have provided incontrovertible evidence of the difficulty I had in thinking up a land use problem. After a delay of about ten seconds, I responded with something like "planned growth and development." She then asked:

Which level of government—state, county, or local—do you think should have primary responsibility for addressing the problem of planned growth?

I responded, although to this day I cannot recall which level of government I mentioned. The interview continued, and about three minutes later the interviewer asked me:

Mr. Asher, what do you think is the second most important land use problem facing Ohio?

This time I really had to struggle for an answer. Finally I uttered triumphantly "sufficient parks and green space." And, of course, the interviewer then asked me which level of government—state, county, or local—should have primary responsibility for rectifying this problem. I gave an answer (which I cannot recall) and said to myself that if the interviewer asked me about the third most important land use problem facing Ohio, I was going to blast her and the entire research project on the grounds that it was measuring nonattitudes. Fortunately for the interviewer, she never asked that question and the interview was completed.

Some months later a report was prepared on the basis of this survey. In the report there appeared statements about which land use problems Ohioans ranked the highest and which levels of government Ohioans wanted to take the lead in addressing these problems. The report made policy recommendations and cited scientific evidence to support its conclusions. As I read the report I got angrier and angrier, for I assumed that most respondents were like me—they gave answers in response to questions but had little information about or interest in land use.

As sponsors of public opinion polls should recognize, not every issue of central importance to them will be an appropriate topic of inquiry within the citizenry at large. Different people have different concerns, and public opinion polls must recognize that fact of life and proceed accordingly.

23

The use of screening questions _____

Steps can be taken in opinion polls to minimize the problem of nonattitudes. The simplest strategy is to make it socially acceptable for respondents to say they are unfamiliar with the topic of the question. This response would result in that question being skipped. Another strategy is to employ screening or filter questions to separate likely attitude holders from nonattitude respondents. With both strategies the intent is to minimize the number of responses that are merely superficial reactions to the interview stimulus. For example, the study cited earlier by Bishop and his colleagues on the fictitious Public Affairs Act employed a variety of screening questions ("Do you have an opinion on this or not?" and "Have you thought much about this issue?") to reduce the frequency of nonattitudes. Respondents who could not pass the screening questions were not asked the Public Affairs Act item.

As another example, the comprehensive study of the American electorate conducted by the Center for Political Studies (CPS) in 1984 utilized a variety of means to lessen the problem of nonattitudes. One item on this 1984 survey asked respondents whether they thought the government in Washington had become too powerful. The exact wording of the question was:

> Some people are afraid the government in Washington is getting too powerful for the good of the country and the individual person. Others feel that the government in Washington is not getting too strong. Do you have an opinion on this or not?

Of the 973 citizens in the sample asked whether they had an opinion, 550 (57 percent) said yes and 423 (43 percent) said no. The sizable 43 percent with no opinion might surprise the reader given the recurring theme of Reagan's presidential victories in 1980 and 1984—namely, the need to reduce the scope and power of the federal government. What this example suggests is that topics hotly discussed by political elites may not be of great importance to the average citizen. In this example, asking people whether or not they had an opinion was a very effective screening question that eliminated about 43 percent of the respondents. One can only speculate as to how many respondents would have answered had the screening question not been used and instead people simply had been asked whether they thought the government was getting too powerful or not. Among the 550 citizens with an opinion on the issue, 311 thought government had gotten too powerful, 218 thought it had not, 10 said it depended, and 11 did not know (even though they had stated in response to the screening question that they

had an opinion on the issue).

Another example of the use of a screening question in the 1984 CPS election study is the following item:

> Some people think the government should provide fewer services, even in areas such as health and education, in order to reduce spending. Suppose these people are at one end of the scale at point number 1. Other people feel it is important for the government to provide many more services even if it means an increase in spending. Suppose these people are at the other end, at point 7. And, of course, some other people have opinions somewhere in between at points 2, 3, 4, 5, or 6. Where would you place yourself on this scale or haven't you thought much about this?

Of the 971 persons asked this question, 150 (about 15 percent) said they had not thought much about the matter. This does not mean that the other 85 percent had thought a lot about the issue and had genuine opinions. The following pattern of responses to this item raises questions about the respondents' answers ($N = 821$):

N	
48	1. Provide many fewer services; reduce spending a lot.
82	2.
141	3.
293	4.
138	5.
58	6.
48	7. Provide many more services; increase spending a lot.
13	Don't know

Note that the largest number of responses ($N = 293$) fall in the middle category 4. This may reflect large numbers of citizens who are satisfied with the status quo or who genuinely take a neutral position on the issue. Or it may reflect the tendency of citizens with genuine, nonneutral preferences on the issue to hide them by opting for the safe middle category. Many responses can be moved out of the middle category if a branching format question is utilized in which citizens who opt for the middle category are then asked whether they favor one side or the other more (Aldrich et al. 1982).

The large number of people in the middle category, however, may signal problems of nonattitudes in the measurement. Perhaps some proportion of people in the middle category place themselves there because they do not want to admit to the interviewer that they haven't thought much about the issue or are unable to place themselves along the scale. Hence, they might choose the middle category as a safe position that makes them seem informed without having to take sides on the issue. If so, then some of the category 4 responses may be nonattitudes rather than genuinely neutral opinions, and the portrait of American public opinion on this issue may be misleading (see p. 30).

In contrast to the pattern of responses on the spending question are citizens' replies to the following item about racial integration:

> Some people think achieving racial integration of schools is so important that it justifies busing children to schools out of their own neighborhoods. Others think letting children go to their own schools is so important that they oppose busing. Where would you place yourself on this scale or haven't you thought much about this?

Here only 69 of 968 respondents (7 percent) said they had not thought much about the issue in contrast to the 15 percent who had not given much thought to the question of government spending. The fact that more people had thought about the busing issue seems intuitively correct since busing on the face of it is more likely to be the kind of issue that hits home and captures citizens' attention. Moreover, the distribution of the busing responses reveals relatively few in the middle category and most responses bunched in the two most antibusing, proneighborhood schools categories ($N = 899$):

N		
33	1.	Bus to achieve integration
15	2.	
25	3.	
70	4.	
91	5.	
186	6.	
462	7.	Keep children in neighborhood schools
17		Don't know

This skewed pattern of responses demonstrates that few Americans are neutral about busing and that the middle category is not the choice for large numbers of citizens with nonattitudes on the issue. It may also be the case that the meaning of a middle position on the busing item is less clear than it is on the previous question of providing services and thus fewer people opt for the middle position.

A final example of a screening question occurs in a 1984 election survey, conducted by the Survey Research Center-Center for Political Studies (SRC-CPS), concerning the use of "feeling thermometers." In essence, the use of the feeling thermometer rests on the ability of people to relate points on a thermometer to degrees of warmth and coldness toward objects. Survey respondents were given the following instructions:

> I'll read the name of a person and I'd like you to rate that person using the feeling thermometer. Ratings between 50 degrees and 100 degrees mean that you feel favorable and warm toward that person. Ratings between 0 degrees and 50 degrees mean that you don't feel much for the person. If we come to a person whose name you don't recognize, you don't need to rate that person. Just tell me and we'll move on to the next name. If you do recognize the name, but you don't feel particularly warm or cold toward the person, you would rate the person at the 50 degree mark.

Ideally, citizens who do not recognize a name or feel that they are unable to evaluate a particular individual would indicate that to the interviewer. However, the instructions to the question itself may encourage respondents to place individuals at the 50 degree mark, including individuals whose names they do not recognize. Table 2-1 indicates the proportion of respondents who gave particular ratings to various political figures. (Keep in mind that Howard Baker was the Senate majority leader at the time of the survey, while Robert Dole was a U.S. senator who would become majority leader the next year.)

The percentage of respondents who do not recognize Ronald Reagan and Walter Mondale or cannot evaluate them is very small, while the comparable percentages for Baker and Dole are much high-

Table 2-1 Thermometer Evaluations of Four Politicians

| Politician | Evaluation | | | | Total percentage (N) |
	Rating other than 50	Rating of 50	Does not recognize	Cannot evaluate	
Reagan	88.3%	10.4%	0 %	1.3%	100% (2,239)
Mondale	79.6	17.7	0.6	2.1	100 (2,239)
Baker	42.0	25.0	25.6	7.4	100 (2,236)
Dole	34.5	29.1	26.8	9.6	100 (2,236)

Source: Survey Research Center-Center for Political Studies, 1984 election study.

Note: Table entries are the percentage of respondents ranking each politician in each category.

er—33 percent and 36.4 percent, respectively. It appears that the screening questions have worked well since more than one-third of the respondents have not rated the less prominent political figures. However, it is disquieting that among the citizens who do assign a thermometer score to these political leaders, many more citizens give a rating of 50 to Baker and Dole than to Reagan and Mondale. Of those citizens evaluating Reagan on the thermometer, only 10.5 percent [10.4/(88.3 + 10.4)] give him a score of 50; the comparable percentage for Mondale is 18.2 [17.7/(79.6 + 17.7)]. But for Baker and Dole, the proportion of citizens using the thermometer who placed them at the midpoint was 37.3 percent [25/(42 + 25)] and 45.8 percent [29.1/(34.5 + 29.1)], respectively.

In one sense it is not surprising that more people placed Baker and Dole at 50; the two Republicans were less well known than Reagan and Mondale in 1984 and therefore more likely to evoke neutral responses. But there may also be a problem of measuring nonattitudes here. The greater frequency of 50 ratings for Baker and Dole may indicate that the screening questions did not eliminate all those persons with no genuine attitudes about the two senators.

An indirect test of this notion is presented in Tables 2-2 and 2-3, which show how education levels and degree of interest in the campaign are related to assigning political figures a thermometer score of 50. One might intuitively expect that citizens with higher levels of education would be able to make more discriminating evaluations and therefore would be less likely to assign thermometer scores of 50. But, as

Table 2-2 Frequency of 50 Ratings of Four Politicians, by Respondents' Education

Politician	Grade school	High school	Some college	College graduate	Post college
Reagan	26.2%	12.8%	5.1%	3.2%	1.7%
Mondale	18.6	20.5	15.4	16.2	16.7
Baker	42.1	38.9	40.3	28.5	29.8
Dole	42.6	46.6	51.4	36.6	39.6

Source: Survey Research Center-Center for Political Studies, 1984 election study.

Note: Table entries are the percentage of respondents assigning a thermometer score who gave the politician in question a score of 50. For example, the 46.6 in the "high school-Dole" category means that 46.6 percent of respondents with a high school education gave Dole a score of 50; the other 53.4 percent of high school respondents assigned Dole a numerical score other than 50.

Table 2-3 Frequency of 50 Ratings of Four Politicians by Respondents' Interest in Campaign

Politician	Very much interested	Somewhat interested	Not very interested
Reagan	7.0%	9.9%	15.9%
Mondale	11.5	17.7	27.7
Baker	25.3	41.4	52.1
Dole	36.9	46.9	59.7

Source: Survey Research Center-Center for Political Studies, 1984 election study.

Note: Table entries are the percentage of respondents assigning a thermometer score who gave the politician in question a score of 50. For example, the 52.1 in the "Baker-not very interested" category means that 52.1 percent of the not very interested respondents who were able to rate Baker gave him a 50, while the other 47.9 percent gave him a score other than 50.

Table 2-2 indicates, this expectation holds only for evaluations of Reagan; for the other three politicians, there is no consistent pattern.

One possible explanation is that low informational levels were so widespread across educational levels, particularly for Baker and Dole, that education did not have a systematic effect on the frequency of nonattitudes. This explanation, if correct, would suggest that many of the scores of 50 represented nonattitudes rather than well thought out positions of neutrality.

Table 2-3 relates the frequency of 50 ratings to the respondents' level of interest in the campaign. As expected, the more interested the respondents, the less likely they are to assign a score of 50 because of their greater awareness of and involvement in the campaign. This pattern holds for all four political leaders. But note that more than one-fourth of the low-interest respondents rated Mondale at 50, while over one-half rated Baker and Dole at that midpoint. These numbers may suggest that little information went into the evaluations of Dole and Baker and again raise the question whether 50 represents a genuine neutral point or simply a convenient and safe home for the expression of nonattitudes that had not been filtered out by the screening questions.

Nonattitudes and the middle position in survey questions

The preceding examples illustrate how difficult it is to assess the magnitude of the nonattitude problem. They also raise another problem

Drawing by C. Barsotti; © 1980 The New Yorker Magazine, Inc.

"I'm undecided, but that doesn't mean I'm apathetic or uninformed."

in attitude and opinion measurement. What does it mean when a person replies to a survey question, "I don't know" or "I can't decide" or "it depends"? Do these responses represent a genuine neutral stance or something else? Should holders of nonattitudes be allowed at the neutral or middle point, or should they be at a distinct point off the measurement scale so as not to create a misleading image of large numbers of citizens thoughtfully adopting the middle position?

The response alternatives included in an item will also affect the extent of nonattitudes. For example, a CBS News/*New York Times* poll conducted in November 1985 asked a national sample of Americans:

"Who should have the most say about what cuts should be made to balance the budget—the President or Congress?" Note that the question did not present respondents with the option that the president and Congress should have equal say. About 4 percent of the sample volunteered this response, but one wonders what percentage of Americans would have opted for this alternative had it been explicitly presented. In marked contrast is the following question asked in a November 1985 ABC News/*Washington Post* poll: "As things presently stand, who do you think is ahead in military power, the United States or the Soviet Union, or do you think they are about the same in military strength?" Twenty-four percent said the United States was ahead, 26 percent the Soviets, 4 percent had no opinion, and 46 percent said that both nations were about the same in military strength. In fact, in the eight times since 1979 that this question has been asked of samples of Americans by ABC News/*Washington Post*, the percentage of respondents citing "the same" has ranged from 34 to 55 with an average of 44. One can only speculate what the responses would have looked like had the middle choice not been provided.

Research has been conducted on the effects of including a middle choice in the response alternatives (Schuman and Presser 1977; Bishop et al. 1980; Presser and Schuman 1980). The inclusion of a middle option typically generates about 25 percent more noncommittal responses. This suggests that the omission of such a choice will result in many substantive responses that are not very meaningful from citizens who have weak to nonexistent attitudes on a subject. In one study Presser and Schuman (1980) administered two forms of a survey item to random subsamples, the only difference between the questions being that a middle alternative was offered on one but not on the other. For example, one item asked about the penalties for using marijuana. It read: "In your opinion, should the penalties for using marijuana be more strict, less strict, or about the same as they are now?" The other version read: "In your opinion, should the penalties for using marijuana be more strict or less strict than they are now?" On average, about 23 percent of the respondents answered "about the same as they are now" when that choice was explicitly included in the question compared with only about 8 percent who volunteered that response when it was not included.

The interpretation of a "don't know" response can be especially problematic since "don't know" can mean many different things (Coombs and Coombs 1976-1977; Faulkenberry and Mason 1978). For some people "don't know" simply reflects the absence of real attitudes on the topic, but for other people it may represent an inability to choose among contending positions. Smith (1984, 229) points out other ways in which "don't know" responses might arise. Respondents may be too insecure to take a stance. Or they may decline to state their opinions out of a strong sense of privacy or because they do not want to offend anybody. Some respondents may want to hasten the completion of the interview by saying "don't know," thereby avoiding follow-up questions. Just as respondents' nonattitudes may be disguised as attitudes, so too their middle responses (including "don't know") may mask genuine attitudes.

Converse (1976-1977) has investigated characteristics of respondents as well as properties of survey questions that might affect the frequency of "no opinion" and "don't know" answers. She found, as expected, that the higher the level of education of respondents the less likely they were to give "no opinion" replies. With respect to question characteristics, she found that the most important feature was the content of the item. As the subject matter of the question became more and more remote from the concerns and interests of citizens, the frequency of "don't know" responses increased.

Is it a good idea to force responses into polar categories and minimize middle or neutral answers? Or is it better to encourage people to choose the middle position? The answer, of course, depends. If people have genuine attitudes, then the public opinion researcher would want those attitudes clearly expressed. The inclusion of a middle category in such a situation might result in cautious citizens opting for the middle position, particularly on controversial issues where they might not want to reveal their true opinions to the interviewer. Yet the exclusion of a middle category might lead people with weak to nonexistent opinions on an issue to choose one of the genuine response options, thereby creating false impressions of genuine attitudes. A similar dilemma occurs with respect to screening questions. One wants to screen out nonattitudes, but one does not want to make it too easy for people to avoid answering questions on which they have real views or make it too difficult to answer when real, albeit weak, attitudes exist.

Hence, we have a problem without a simple, neat solution. The public opinion pollster and the consumer of the research must simply be sensitive to whether and in what form screening questions were used. They must also be aware of the response alternatives provided to the respondents. Finally, the appropriateness of particular substantive questions to particular samples of citizens should always be a central concern of the political analyst and the public opinion consumer. This latter point is well illustrated in the next section on the stability of survey responses in the context of nonattitudes.

The "mushiness index"

If one is measuring genuine attitudes in a survey, then one would normally expect some reasonable degree of stability in these responses over time. Yet in many instances survey responses fluctuate wildly over a relatively short period, which raises questions about how real the measured opinions were in the first place. In response to this phenomenon the polling firm of Yankelovich, Skelly and White developed the "mushiness index." The index was designed to assess the volatility in the public's views on issues, particularly those issues about which citizens have little information and understanding yet provide answers to pollsters' questions. The mushiness index has four components in addition to a person's position on a particular issue: how much the issue affects the respondent personally, how well informed the respondent feels on the issue, how much the respondent discusses the issue with family and friends, and the respondent's own assessment of how likely his or her views on the issue will change (Keene and Sackett 1981). On the basis of these criteria, Yankelovich, Skelly and White placed issues into three categories ranging from very volatile, or "mushy," to firm and found in general that attitudes on domestic policy were less mushy than those on foreign policy.

The usefulness of the mushiness index was illustrated by the following example (Keene and Sackett 1981, 51). A sample of Americans was asked: "Do you favor or oppose restricting imports of foreign goods such as Japanese cars, textiles and steel, which are less expensive than American products?" Fifty-four percent favored restricting imports, 41 percent opposed restrictions, and only 5 percent were unsure. But when the sample was broken down into three groups according to the mushiness criteria, the patterns of response were quite different. Among the mushiest group, 39 percent favored restrictions, 37 percent opposed them, and 24 percent were unsure; among the firmest group, 62 percent favored restrictions, 37 percent opposed them, and 1 percent was unsure.

Respondents' knowledge about an issue (one component of the mushiness index) affects their attitudes as an April 1986 CBS News/ *New York Times* poll made clear. The poll queried Americans about their support for the Nicaraguan contras, rebels fighting against the Sandinista government. Overall 25 percent of the sample was willing to give aid to the contras, while 62 percent opposed it. But when the sample was divided according to whether the respondents knew which side the United States supported in Nicaragua, major differences were observed (Shipler 1986). Among those respondents who were aware of which side the United States favored, 40 percent supported aid to the contras, and 52 percent opposed it. But for those who were not aware of American policy, only 16 percent favored contra aid, while 59 percent opposed such assistance.

The mushiness index is not widely used in surveys, in part because it is too costly and time consuming to ask all the questions needed to construct the index, particularly when multiple substantive issues are covered in the survey. Nevertheless, the concept of mushiness is of interest analytically since it helps explain a number of apparent anomalies in American public opinion. One puzzle is the rapid swings in public opinion often observed after the president of the United States delivers a speech on a single issue, particularly foreign policy. Public opinion is most volatile on issues that seem distant in terms of their likely effects on people and their susceptibility to citizen influence. We often praise the president for his ability to move public opinion, not recognizing that on some issues a somewhat mindless "follow the leader" mentality is at work; the president would be successful in moving public opinion in any direction, assuming he is able to portray the issue in ways beneficial to his own objectives.

The rationale underlying the mushiness index is not new to Yankelovich, Skelly and White; almost forty years ago George Gallup (1947) espoused survey designs that measured multiple aspects of a person's opinion. Indeed, Schuman and Presser (1981) and other investigators have stressed the need to measure the importance of an issue to a person as well as his or her opinion on that issue in order to better understand the dynamics of attitude change. However, Yankelovich, Skelly and White had the public relations acumen to coin a catchy phrase for their work which built on the findings of earlier public opinion studies.

Many survey questions seem to be prime candidates for high mushiness scores, yet unfortunately these scores will not be calculable since the necessary follow-up questions were not asked because of insufficient time and space on the survey. Thus, poll users need to ask themselves whether the topic of the survey is likely to be of concern to the respondents or whether it is more of an abstraction with little immediate and practical relevance. If the former, mushiness and nonattitudes are not likely to be a serious problem. The complicating factor is that the topic of the survey is likely to be of varying importance to different segments of the American population. Unemployed steel and auto workers are more likely to be concerned about foreign imports and thus have more stable attitudes on the issue. Likewise, senior citizens are more likely to have well-developed views on Social Security and

Medicare. American public opinion on a particular issue includes rather divergent views of various subgroups of the population, some of whom have genuine attitudes on the issue, while others do not. Moreover, in trying to relate public opinion to the processes and decisions of government, the whole of public opinion may be less important than the opinion of a particular subset of people. It may be that on certain issues, it is the views of a few people with genuine attitudes that will have the greatest impact on government policy and policy makers.

Conclusion

The problem of nonattitudes remains one of the least considered aspects of public opinion polling. Other facets of public opinion research such as question wording and sampling receive much more attention, even to the point of being mentioned in television and newspaper reports of public opinion poll results. But very few people raise the most fundamental question of all: Was the topic of the survey of interest to the respondents? Did the poll query people on subjects about which they held genuine views?

As discussed earlier, assessing the actual magnitude of nonattitudes is a very difficult task that is made even more troublesome by the tendency of people to respond to questions not in terms of their actual intent and content, but in terms of the cues provided by the questions and whatever meaning (often idiosyncratic) that they read into them. For example, a person asked whether he or she favored giving foreign aid to Chad might answer the question, not on the basis of any information about Chad, but on the basis of a predisposition toward foreign aid in general. Likewise, citizens asked whether they favored joint American-Soviet space ventures might respond on the basis of their underlying view of the Soviet Union rather than on the basis of concrete views about the optimal way to explore outer space. The pressures in an interview situation to provide an answer may lead respondents to seek out whatever cues are available in order to answer the question. Because of the absence of attitudes about the topic, citizens may impute a variety of meanings to the question to come up with a response.

The problem of nonattitudes should not lead one to disregard polls because on many issues the general public has genuine attitudes and is willing and able to express them. There are other issues on which only a small subset of the public may have real opinions, but even then events may transform such an issue from one followed by only a small part of the citizenry to one that engages the serious attention of the mass public. Public opinion polls do provide valid assessments of what Americans are thinking; one should simply keep in mind that not all issues are appropriate topics for public opinion surveys.

Nonattitudes are more a problem of the respondent than of the measuring instrument. That is, nonattitudes can arise even when a question is carefully constructed without any loaded words or implied alternatives. The best of questions can still result in the measurement of nonattitudes. Nevertheless, deficiencies in the questions themselves can contribute to the problem of nonattitudes as well as to many other difficulties encountered in public opinion polling. Thus, we now turn to a discussion of how question wording, question order, and question context can affect the results of public opinion polls.

Note

1. I am using the terms *attitude* and *opinion* interchangeably. Many social scientists differentiate between attitudes and opinions by treating the latter as more transitory, as verbal representations of some underlying attitude. That is, an opinion is viewed as a verbal manifestation of an attitude that is elicited by the public opinion survey. For the purposes of this chapter, this distinction is by no means critical, although the reader should recognize that public opinion data at times may simply be verbal responses (opinions) that we hope accurately reflect some underlying attitudes.

Wording and context of questions 3

Of all the potential problem areas of public opinion polling, question wording is probably the most familiar to the consumer of public opinion research. Common sense tells us that the use of a loaded word or an inflammatory phrase can affect the pattern of responses to a survey question. If one wants a poll to show weak support for federal assistance to financially beleaguered entities (such as New York City in the 1970s or the Lockheed and Chrysler corporations), all one need do is ask Americans whether they favor a federal "bailout" of these entities. Few people favor a bailout, but many more support federal loans with proper safeguards that the monies will be repaid. Or if one wants a poll to indicate scant support for providing foreign aid, all one need do is construct an argumentative and leading question such as: Do you favor giving foreign aid to other nations when there are children in the United States who are suffering from hunger? To demonstrate support for foreign aid, one would load the question differently: Do you favor giving foreign aid to other nations in order to help them resist communist subversion and thereby enhance our national security?

Obviously, individuals and groups with an ax to grind can easily construct questions that will generate desired responses. The response alternatives they provide to the interviewees can also help them achieve the intended result. Certainly, if a middle alternative is not listed as one of the choices, then fewer citizens will opt for that choice, and this can alter the interpretation of a poll. For example, if a mayor wanted a poll to indicate support for the city's spending policies in the area of garbage collection, he might construct this question: Do you think the city of _____ is spending too much, too little, or about the right amount on garbage collection? Clearly, the response "about the right amount" is an endorsement of the mayor's current policies. If "about the right

39

amount" was not included as an explicit response alternative, fewer such replies would result because citizens would have to volunteer that response. This, in turn, would create a portrait of greater citizen dissatisfaction with the mayor's spending on garbage collection.

Thus, bad question wording may occur when polls are conducted by interested parties whose aim is to generate specific responses. Yet most professional polls have not been blatantly manipulated; instead, questions are typically worded in a nonbiased, fair, and straightforward fashion. But as we shall soon demonstrate, even when there is no obvious ax to grind, question wording choices can be very consequential to the results obtained. There are many instances in which highly reputable polling organizations have arrived at very divergent conclusions simply because they employed different (albeit good) questions on a particular topic.

Less obvious than the impact of question wording is the effect on responses of the order and/or context in which specific questions are placed. A typical public opinion survey includes many questions, and the placement of a particular question can affect the responses to that item. Yet most consumers of public opinion research know little about item order and therefore have little sense of how the context has shaped the responses.

Consider the following hypothetical example. Imagine a survey assessing popular attitudes toward negotiating with the Soviet Union. The key question measuring support for negotiations is preceded by a battery of items about Soviet-sponsored terrorism and the Soviet invasion of Afghanistan. The perceived efficacy of negotiations will be diminished by the previous questions that probably put the respondents in a more hostile frame of mind toward the Soviet Union. Or imagine a survey in which the popularity of the president is measured after a series of questions dealing with scandals in his administration and difficulties with the economy and the Congress. Certainly, reactions to the president will be more negative when respondents are first reminded of these problems. The point of both examples is that the context in which a particular survey item is embedded can help shape responses to that item.

This chapter will present numerous examples from a variety of real-world settings. It will become clear, if it is not so already, that some "question effects" are obvious and therefore less likely to mislead the citizen, while others are subtle and more troublesome and may indeed manipulate and mislead the unsuspecting consumer of public opinion research.

40

Question wording

More than three decades ago Stanley Payne wrote *The Art of Asking Questions*. In the last chapter he presented a check list of 100 considerations organized around themes such as the topic being studied, the structure of the question and the response alternatives, the treatment of the respondents, the words themselves, sources of bias, and the readability of the questions. Most of what Payne said then still holds today and demonstrates that much of what is involved in constructing good questions is common sense (Payne 1951).

Yet common sense is often in short supply. Seemingly straightforward questions that employ relatively simple language can seem ambiguous to the respondent. Even simple questions about the number of persons in a household or the number of children in a family can present difficulties. For example, in surveys in which the wife and husband were both interviewed independently, their responses did not agree perfectly about such "factual" items as the number of children they had (Asher 1974b). Perhaps errors were made in transcribing their responses. Or perhaps there was ambiguity in the question itself. One spouse might have responded in terms of children living at home, the other in terms of the total number. Or one spouse might have included children from a previous marriage, while the other might not have.

Measurement of a respondent's age has also proven to be surprisingly problematic. Peterson (1984) showed that four different ways of measuring age in a survey yielded substantially different refusal rates, although the age data obtained were very similar across the four formats.

If question wording can affect measurement of objective matters such as age and the number of children in a family, then how extensive might wording effects be on more subjective phenomena? The answer, of course, is that wording can make a great difference. For example, Sussman (1985i) reports on three different versions of a question used in ABC News/*Washington Post* surveys to measure the public's attitudes toward President Ronald Reagan's Strategic Defense Initiative (SDI), commonly known as "Star Wars." In 1983 the survey asked Americans if they had "heard or read of a proposal by Reagan that the United States develop defensive military weapons using lasers and particle beams to shoot down enemy missiles." It then queried, "Well, do you favor or oppose developing such defensive weapons, or what?" In this survey 65 percent knew of SDI. Fifty-four percent were in favor, 37 percent opposed, and 9 percent undecided.

41

A July 1985 poll began by telling respondents that SDI weapons "could destroy nuclear missiles fired at the United States by the Soviet Union or other countries." It then stated,

> Supporters say such weapons could guarantee protection of the United States from nuclear attack and are worth whatever they cost. Opponents say such weapons will not work, will increase the arms race, and that the research will cost many billions of dollars. How about you: Would you say you approve of plans to develop such space-based weapons?

Here the results were 41 percent in favor, 53 percent opposed, and 6 percent undecided, a pattern far different from the 1983 results.

Because the July version of the survey included two positive and three negative arguments, a third version of the question was tried in October 1985 that omitted the clause "such weapons will not work." The results of this version were 48 percent in favor, 46 percent opposed, and 6 percent undecided. Different question wording yielded different results, although some of the differences may have been due to genuine changes in attitudes over the time period in which the questions were asked.

One can cite innumerable examples of the impact of question wording on responses. In 1982 the Advisory Commission on Intergovernmental Relations sponsored three surveys asking Americans which services they would cut if funds were short (Herbers 1982). Respondents were asked, "Suppose the budgets of your state and local governments have to be curtailed, which of these parts would you limit most severely?" About 8 percent of the respondents cited "aid to the needy" when that response was listed as one of the service areas that could be cut. But when the term "public welfare programs" was used in place of "aid to the needy" and the other choices remained the same, many more respondents (39 percent) opted to cut welfare. Obviously, aid to the needy is much more popular than public welfare, and the program label used in the survey strongly influenced the results. It has been a common phenomenon for the American public to complain about welfare in general, but to be highly supportive of specific programs that could justifiably be included under the rubric of welfare.

Two 1986 polls conducted in Great Britain on Britons' attitudes toward their country's nuclear force illustrate how consequential the slightest variations in question wording can be (Lelyveld 1986, 2E). When a Gallup poll asked Britons whether their nuclear force made them feel "safe," 40 percent said yes and 50 percent said no. But when a Marplan poll conducted at a similar time asked whether their nuclear force made them feel "safer," 50 percent responded yes and only 36 percent no. Clearly, the choice of "safe" or "safer" changes the meaning of the question.

Poll results about presidential preference in 1980 provide another example of the importance of question wording (Townley 1980). In May 1980 an NBC News poll asked a sample of citizens an open-ended question about whom they would like to see elected in 1980; the question did not mention any specific candidates. The leading choice was "not sure" with 25 percent, followed by Carter and Reagan, each with 24 percent, and John Anderson far back at 5 percent. A week later a Harris poll asked likely voters, "If you had to choose right now, would you vote for Reagan, Carter or Anderson?" This time the results were 39 percent for Reagan, 34 percent for Carter, 24 percent for Anderson, and only 5 percent undecided. It is highly unlikely that any political event in the week between the two polls caused these highly discrepant results. Instead, the explanation must lie with question wording and the fact that one question specifically mentioned candidates and the other did not.

Two June 1978 polls that included questions about U.S.-Soviet relations provide another example of the importance of question wording. A Harris poll asked Americans, "Do you favor or oppose détente—that is the United States and Russia seeking out areas of agreement and cooperation?" Sixty-nine percent favored détente, and 19 percent opposed it. But when a CBS News/*New York Times* poll asked, "What do you think the U.S. should do—should the U.S. try harder to relax tensions with the Russians or instead should it get tougher in its dealings with the Russians?" only 30 percent said relax tensions, and 53 percent said get tougher. One might argue that these two sets of results are not really contradictory because the questions do not measure the same thing. However, because the investigator has tremendous leeway in deciding how to frame questions about a particular subject, it is important to recognize that two ostensibly similar questions generated highly divergent results.

Often in providing the respondent with some background within which to answer a question, a pollster may go too far. In a June 17, 1985, editorial entitled "A Grain of Salt, Please," the *Washington Post* complained about the increasingly common practice of informing respondents about a topic in order to ascertain their opinion on it. Obviously, the content of the information provided to the respondents will have a lot to do with their subsequent views on the issue. The *Post* editorial cited an example from a Harris poll that demonstrated how ludicrous

FRANK AND ERNEST ©by Bob Thaves

IT SEEMS TO ME THAT "HOW MANY IN YOUR HOUSEHOLD?" WOULD BE A SIMPLE QUESTION TO ANSWER, DR. JEKYLL.

matters can become. The following agree-disagree statement was presented to a sample of Americans in January 1985: "When Goetz said in his confession that he used dum-dum bullets, that he was sorry he didn't gouge out the eyes of the four he shot, and that if he could have reloaded his gun fast enough, he would have taken out after them, he looks more like a 'Death Wish' gunman out stalking to kill criminals, not an innocent victim just trying to defend himself." As the *Post* opined, "The wonder is not that a majority agreed with the statement, but that 38 percent of the respondents had the gumption to disagree."

My favorite example of an argumentative question purporting to inform the respondent occurred in the 1982 Democratic primary for governor in Ohio. There were three major candidates running—the former lieutenant governor Richard Celeste, the incumbent attorney general William Brown, and the former mayor of Cincinnati Jerry Springer. The pollster for the attorney general (Pat Caddell's Cambridge Survey Research) included the following question in a statewide survey:

> As you may know, in 1974, Jerry Springer, who had gotten married six months earlier, was arrested on a morals charge with three women in a hotel room. He also used a bad check to pay for the women's services, and subsequently resigned as mayor of his city. Does this make you much more likely, somewhat more likely, somewhat less likely, or much less likely to support Jerry Springer for governor this year?

In addition to being factually incorrect on a number of points, this question was a blatant effort by the pollster to provide information that would generate negative responses to a candidate and then to use the replies in a highly selective and political way. In the context of our discussion of nonattitudes in Chapter 2, this was an attempt to create attitudes on the basis of the interview situation. This can be done in a variety of ways. One is to present hypothetical situations to citizens and then ask them to react to these situations. More often than not, the information obtained is of dubious utility because the hypothetical situations have forced the respondents into a world that has little real meaning for them.

Sometimes questions are worded properly, but the responses are misinterpreted, a problem that will be discussed more extensively in Chapter 8. An example from public opinion on the Vietnam war will help clarify this point. During the war Americans were regularly asked their views about the bombing of North Vietnam. When majorities were recorded in favor of the bombing, supporters of the war interpreted that to mean Americans wanted a military and not a diplomatic solution. Likewise, when strong support was indicated for negotiating with the North Vietnamese, "dovish" Americans used that to argue a military solution was not supported by Americans. Either interpretation may be right or wrong. However, there is nothing at all inconsistent about supporting both bombing and negotiating if one's top priority is to end the war as quickly as possible. The political analyst must be careful not to impose his or her interpretive framework on the public's responses to survey questions. The average citizen may be operating in a cognitively different world in which ideas are linked together in ways quite surprising to the pundit and the pollster. Knowing what a person is against doesn't necessarily reveal the reasons for that position nor does it automatically indicate what the person is for.

A final aspect of question wording is the use of multiple questions to measure some topic and the combination of the responses to these questions into an index or scale. Often no single questionnaire item can adequately measure the multifaceted construct that the public opinion analyst is studying. Hence, a series of questions may be asked and the results combined into an index. For example, *political efficacy* is a concept that has been of great interest to political scientists (Asher 1974a). It refers to a citizen's feelings of effectiveness in dealing with government.

© Reprinted with special permission of King Features Syndicate, Inc.

Early measures of political efficacy generally relied upon four statements:

1. I don't think public officials care much what people like me think.
2. Voting is the only way that people like me can have any say about how the government runs things.
3. Sometimes politics and government seem so complicated that a person like me can't really understand what's going on.
4. People like me don't have any say about what the government does.

These items are usually included in surveys in an agree-disagree format with a disagree response representing the efficacious position on all four items. An efficacy index could be constructed by simply counting the number of items to which the respondent gave an efficacious answer. This number could range from zero to four; respondents who gave three or four efficacious responses might be classified as high in efficacy, two efficacious answers as medium in efficacy, and zero or one efficacious reply as low in efficacy.

The use of an index is justified on both substantive and methodological grounds (Asher 1974c). Substantively, the index does a better job representing the complexity of the concept being studied than any single item could. Methodologically, the use of a multiple-item index can be beneficial in lessening the harmful effects of the random measurement error that is present in survey data. However, the consumer of public opinion polls is often not provided sufficient information about the components of the index including the actual wording of the questions. Moreover, the ways in which the separate items relate to each other and how they are combined into an index may not be explained to the poll user. Hence, the citizen often must accept on faith that the index has been constructed properly from individual items that themselves were appropriately worded. Chapter 8 presents some substantive examples of situations in which multiple items on a topic were available for analysis.

Question order and context _____

Question order can dramatically affect responses to survey items by altering the framework and context within which the question is answered. An excellent example of the impact of question order occurred in 1980 when the Harris organization employed a "double vote" question to measure citizens' candidate preferences in the presidential primaries. The Harris organization asked respondents at the beginning of the interview whether they intended to vote for President Jimmy Carter or Senator Edward M. Kennedy in the hotly contested nomination battle. Next followed questions about domestic and foreign policy, including items about inflation and the economy, American hostages in Iran, and the Soviet invasion of Afghanistan. Toward the end of the interview, the sample was again asked its likely vote intention. Surprisingly, over the course of the interview support for President Carter declined sharply. The only explanation for this drop was that as respondents thought about Carter's record, their views of Carter became more negative.

A similar phenomenon occurred in an ABC News/*Washington Post* study of the placement of a presidential popularity question in a survey (Sussman 1984a). In November 1983 a sample of Americans was asked the presidential popularity question twice, once at the beginning of the interview and again at the end with a variety of issue questions in between. Unlike the preceding Kennedy versus Carter example, there was very little difference in the overall distribution of the responses at the two time points. Initially, 59 percent approved of the president's performance, 37 percent disapproved, and 4 percent had no opinion. Later, 59 percent approved, 39 percent disapproved, and 2 percent had no opinion. However, more than 15 percent of the sample changed their opinion about the president over the course of the twenty-minute interview, with 8 percent moving from approval to disapproval and 7 percent moving the opposite way. An experimental study by Sigelman (1981) yielded similar results. The distribution of responses to the presidential popularity item was barely affected by the placement of the question within the overall survey. However, the willingness of people to provide an evaluation of the president, be it positive or negative, was affected by the placement of the popularity item; asking the question at the beginning of the survey resulted in a smaller proportion of respondents offering an evaluation of presidential popularity, an effect particularly pronounced among persons with low levels of education.

In early 1984 the major national polls were yielding highly divergent results in a presidential trial heat between Ronald Reagan and Walter Mondale (Sussman 1984b). A CBS News/*New York Times* poll showed Reagan beating Mondale by 48 to 32 percent; two other polls showed the race to be much closer, Gallup calling it even and the ABC News/*Washington Post* poll showing Reagan ahead by three points.

The discrepancy among the three polls was largely attributed to the placement of the trial heat questions. The latter two polls asked the vote intention question at the end of the interview, while the CBS News/ *New York Times* survey asked it at the beginning. It was argued that asking the question at the beginning benefited the president since he was so much better known than Mondale, while asking it after a battery of questions on troublesome issues lessened the president's advantage.

The effects of question wording and context have been extensively researched. A major book by Schuman and Presser (1981) demonstrated that question order effects were prominent, particularly on general, somewhat amorphous questions that have little direct relevance to respondents. They warned that in examining the distribution of responses to identical questions asked at multiple points in time, one must take into account whether the context in which the questions were asked was also identical. The significance of this point was supported by the work of Bishop, Oldendick, and Tuchfarber (1982) who argued that the decline in Americans' level of political interest uncovered in a 1978 survey was partly due to changes in the context and order in which the political interest question was asked; the real decline in political interest was not nearly as worrisome as originally thought.

A 1984 study by Bishop, Oldendick, and Tuchfarber found that respondents' reports of how much they follow government and politics depend on the context in which the question is asked. For example, if respondents are asked how much they follow government and public affairs after they are asked some difficult questions about their knowledge of their representative's record, they are likely to lower their estimate of their attentiveness to politics. But if respondents are first asked about their attentiveness to politics, they tend to assert a higher level of interest.

The works of Eubank and Gow (1983) and Gow and Eubank (1984) further illustrate the effects of question order and context. They examined the 1978, 1980, and 1982 American National Election Studies, which are national sample surveys of Americans that political scientists have used extensively to study the effects of incumbency in citizens' vote choices in U.S. House elections. Political scientists have found that incumbency is a very strong factor in voting, but Eubank and Gow argue that this finding is somewhat artificial due to the placement of questions in the American National Election Studies. They point out that prior to being asked their vote for Congress, respondents are asked a series of questions about their incumbent U.S. representative. This sequencing of questions makes it more likely that respondents will claim to have voted for the incumbent when they in fact did not, a tendency especially pronounced among less knowledgeable citizens who are more suscepti- ble to the effects of question order.

The ability of one question to affect responses to another has been demonstrated by Hyman and Sheatsley (1950), Schuman and Presser (1981), and Schuman, Kalton, and Ludwig (1983). Their studies have examined responses to the following two items:

> Do you think the United States should let Communist newspaper reporters from other countries come in here and send back to their papers the news as they see it?

> Do you think a Communist country like Russia should let American newspaper reporters come in and send back to America the news as they see it?

When these two questions are asked in the preceding order, support for letting communist reporters come to the United States is much lower than when the questions are asked in the reverse order. The explanation for this pattern seems clear: it is difficult for the respondent to deny communist reporters the opportunity to come to the United States if they have already said that American reporters should be allowed to go to Russia. This effect of context is strong when the questions are contiguous in a survey, but the effect remains strong even when the items are separated by many other questions.

A final example of context effects is provided by Schuman, Presser, and Ludwig (1981). They studied the consequences of different order- ings of a general and a specific question on abortion. The items read:

> Do you think it should be possible for a pregnant woman to obtain a le- gal abortion if she is married and does not want any more children? [general]

> Do you think it should be possible for a pregnant woman to obtain a le- gal abortion if there is a strong chance of serious defect in the baby? [specific]

The authors found that responses to the general item were very much influenced by whether the item came first or second, while responses to the specific question were not affected by item order. More specifically, support for abortion in general was much higher when the general item came first. Their explanation for this finding, although speculative, suggests the kinds of cognitive calculations that may shape a response:

> One plausible explanation for the effect turns on the fact that there are a number of different reasons for supporting legalized abortion. A possible defect in an unborn child is a specific reason that appeals to a

49

large part of the population. When the more general item is asked first, some respondents may say yes but mainly with such a specific reason in mind. When the item on abortion because of a defective child is asked first, however, this indicates to respondents that the general item which follows does not refer to that specific case. Thus respondents who are reluctant to favor abortion except within narrow limits should find it easier to oppose the general rationale after having favored (and "subtracted") the more specific rationale about the defective child. (Schuman, Presser, and Ludwig 1981, 220).

In contrast to the communist reporters' example in which a particular question order promoted consistency, here a particular ordering generated divergence in the sense that some respondents favored abortion in the specific case but opposed it more generally.

In addition to the ordering of specific survey items among other questions, context refers to the substantive framework within which questions are placed. Pollsters can choose the framework within which they ask questions, and this choice can be very consequential. A survey about the American military buildup posed in the context of Soviet military strength would probably elicit more supportive attitudes toward defense spending than would a similar survey framed in the context of the huge national debt. In their work on white Americans' attitudes toward affirmative action, Kinder and Sanders (1986) found clear differences in the correlates and antecedents of opinion depending upon whether the questions were presented in the context of reverse discrimination (affirmative action discriminates against whites) or in the context of undeserved advantage (affirmative action gives blacks advantages they haven't earned). For example, white opinions were more racially motivated when affirmative action was placed in the context of undeserved advantage.

Finally, context can refer to the broader environment in which the interview is occurring. Personal circumstances, recent societal events, and the content of media coverage can alter the meaning of a survey question for a respondent. An identically worded question can mean dramatically different things to respondents depending upon the frame of reference they bring to the interview situation. And one part of that frame of reference will be the social and political context extant at the time of the interview.

Conclusion

Citizens are in a better position to evaluate the effects of question wording than they are to assess the consequences of question order for a number of reasons. First, much of what is involved in question wording is common sense; people can often sense when a question is worded in a misleading and loaded fashion. More importantly, when public opinion results are reported, the wording of the particular questions is often provided. Thus, citizens have the opportunity to form their own judgments about the quality of the question wording. But the consumer of polling is given no information whatsoever in newspaper and television reports about the overall structure and content of the survey, although the major news organizations are very willing to mail the complete report of a poll to interested citizens. Hence, citizens normally do not have any basis to form independent judgments about whether their responses to a particular item have been affected by its placement within the questionnaire. Moreover, the effects of question order and context are likely to be more subtle, thereby making it more difficult for citizens to assess these effects even when the text of the complete survey instrument is provided.

Fortunately, polling organizations are becoming more sensitive to the consequences of question order, and survey research textbooks are at last addressing the problem in more detail. Today reputable pollsters give more attention to context effects and are more likely to inform the consumers of their polls about the potential consequences of question order. Nevertheless, it remains quite easy for the unscrupulous pollster, intent upon generating a preferred response to a particular question, to mislead and manipulate the public by embedding that question in the survey so as to yield the desired answer.

Sampling techniques ⎯⎯⎯ 4

Of all the aspects of public opinion polling, sampling generates the greatest skepticism among Americans. One source of this skepticism is the actual composition of the sample as reflected in the plaintive question "How come no one has asked me about my opinion on that issue?" An experience I had in October 1984 exemplifies Americans' suspicion of polls. I was to make a presentation on the 1984 presidential election before a group of about seventy labor union leaders. During his introduction of me, the president of the Ohio AFL-CIO, obviously upset with national polls showing Democratic nominee Walter Mondale badly trailing President Ronald Reagan, conducted his own two-part poll. He first asked the audience how many were for Mondale and how many were for Reagan. Everyone was for Mondale. He next asked how many people in the audience had been interviewed by the national pollsters concerning their presidential preference. None had. He then concluded by expressing disdain for the entire enterprise of polling. After that inauspicious introduction, he turned the platform over to me so that I might give my poll-based analysis of the 1984 campaign.

Although not a statistical explanation of sample selection, this chapter will cover a number of aspects of sampling so that the consumer of public opinion research will better understand how and why samples are selected. The first topic will be a nontechnical review of various sampling designs followed by a brief discussion of some factors that affect sample size. Then sampling error and confidence levels will be discussed from the perspective of how they relate to the interpretation of poll results. The chapter concludes with a discussion of total sample size versus actual sample size. Too often reports of poll results pay little attention to the actual number of cases on which a conclusion is based, a number that can be substantially smaller than the total sample size.

Sampling designs _____

The aim of a good sampling design is to select a sample that is appropriate for the research topic and within the investigator's budget. Because it is impossible to interview everyone within a population—whether the population of the United States, of New York, of all doctors, or whatever—a sample of that population is selected. The key requirement of the sample is that it enables one to generalize from the sample results to the broader population from which the sample was drawn. Typically, the sample is of interest because of what it reveals about the overall population and not because of the actual sample characteristics themselves. Hence, ways are needed to select samples that accurately reflect the broader population from which they are drawn. This can be done in a variety of ways depending on the nature of the respondents, the objectives of the research, and the resources available to the investigator.

All of the designs to be discussed are examples of *probability sampling*, the dominant and preferred mode of sampling public opinion. Probability samples have a number of advantages. The foremost are that they tend to be more representative than other kinds of samples and that they permit the calculation of a quantity called the *sampling error* (discussed later in the chapter), which enables one to estimate with a certain level of confidence how discrepant the sample results are from the true population values. The defining characteristic of a probability sample is the ability to determine the probability of any single person being selected in the sample.

There are many examples of nonprobability sampling. The television reporter who does a number of "man on the street" interviews to assess public opinion on an issue has actually selected a nonprobability sample. There is no way of telling how representative these interviewees are or how accurate the sample results are. Radio call-in surveys are also based on nonprobability samples; the callers may or may not be representative of the larger community. Likewise, the questionnaires mailed by U.S. representatives to all the households in their districts exemplify a nonprobability sampling procedure. Thousands of questionnaires may be returned, but there is no assurance that they constitute an accurate sample of the district.

Random and systematic sampling

The chief requirement for random sampling, one method of probability sampling, is a list or enumeration of the persons in the overall population. If one has such a list, then the actual process of sampling is straightforward. A unique number is assigned to each person, and then a sample of these numbers is selected. A primitive way of selecting the sample would be to put all the numbers in a hat, mix them up, and then draw the sample. A more likely method would be to use a table of random numbers or computer-generated random numbers to select the sample. This kind of sampling technique is appropriate when a reasonably complete and current listing of the population is available.

Random sampling of individuals is not a feasible way to select a national sample of Americans for a number of reasons. First, there is no good list of all Americans. But even if there were, random sampling would not be useful, particularly if one were planning to interview the respondents personally rather than on the telephone. A randomly selected national sample would require sending interviewers all over the country, which would make the cost of the poll prohibitive. Hence, cluster sampling techniques (discussed later) have been developed to select samples from large geographical areas when personal interviewing is to be used.

Systematic sampling is a variant of random sampling in which one picks every Nth name from the list after picking the first name at random. For example, to select a sample of 500 students from a student directory of 25,000 names (a 2 percent or one-fiftieth sample), one might first pick at random a number between one and fifty. Suppose that number were twelve. Then the sample would consist of the twelfth name in the directory, the sixty-second name, and every fiftieth name thereafter.

Systematic sampling is easily done; the only caveat is that the listing of the names should have no cycle or periodicity to it lest the skip interval coincide with the periodicity. Normally, names listed in alphabetical order present no problems whatsoever. An example of a problematic list would be one in which male and female names alternated. Depending upon whether the skip interval was an even or odd number, the sample would be composed entirely of males or of females, thus introducing a bias to the study. Another example of a periodicity problem might be a list of homes within a major housing development. If one were picking a sample of homes in order to interview the owners, one would want to ensure that there was no special pattern to the listing of homes. For example, suppose every tenth home on the list was on a corner lot. If by chance one selected a sample that included only corner homes, this could introduce a serious bias to the study since corner-lot homes tend to be larger and more expensive and thus owned by wealthier persons than homes within the block.

Stratified sampling

The key characteristic of stratified sampling is that the population is divided into subsets or strata according to some characteristics of interest to the investigator. After the population has been stratified, one might then sample randomly or systematically within the strata. For example, to interview a sample of members of the U.S. House of Representatives, one might first stratify the members according to their political party affiliation (Democratic versus Republican) and their seniority (for simplicity, high versus low), two characteristics of relevance to the research, rather than pick a random sample. This stratification creates four categories: high seniority Democrats, low seniority Democrats, high seniority Republicans, and low seniority Republicans. One would then sample within each of the strata.

In order to stratify the population, one must have knowledge of the characteristics of the individuals in the population. Stratification guarantees that the sample will include a sufficient number of cases with the characteristics of interest to the researcher. The major advantages of stratified sampling are a reduction in sampling error and a guarantee of representativeness with respect to the variables used in stratifying.

Cluster sampling

Cluster sampling entails multiple interviews within the same geographical area, typically a neighborhood. The advantage of cluster sampling is economic. It is expensive to support an interviewer in the field and to get that interviewer to a particular site to conduct an interview. The cost would be made more manageable if the interviewer could conduct multiple interviews at that site.

Cluster sampling is usually part of a multistage sampling scheme employed by organizations that wish to interview personally a national sample of Americans. For example, the Survey Research Center of the University of Michigan utilizes multistage sampling; at all stages except the last, geographical areas, not individuals, are sampled. Typically, the sample design selects a sample of counties; then a sample of cities, townships, and unincorporated areas within the sample of counties; then a sample of city blocks and/or land tracts from the sample of cities, townships, and unincorporated areas; and then a sample of residential dwellings that are located on the sampled blocks and land tracts. For example, Cook County might be included in the sample of counties. Then Chicago might be selected within Cook County. Then a number of blocks would be selected from within Chicago, and then some dwelling units would be chosen from the selected blocks.

Note that to this stage geographical units and not individuals have been sampled. Sampling geographical units is relatively straightforward. It is easy to pick a sample of counties and a sample of localities within the counties; lists of counties and municipalities are readily available. Likewise, it is fairly easy to pick samples of blocks and dwelling units since such information is kept by local governments for the purpose of tax assessment. At each step in the typical multistage design, the probability of a geographical unit being included in the sample is proportional to its population. Thus, Cook County and Los Angeles County are almost certain to be included in the sample of counties, while sparsely populated rural counties will have very little chance of being included. A sample concentrated in the major metropolitan areas of the country helps keep the cost of supporting and transporting interviewing staff reasonable.

Once the interviewer (usually a woman) arrives at the selected dwelling unit, she refers to instructions provided to her to determine whom to interview; it is not left to the interviewer's discretion to decide whom to interview. These instructions are usually couched in terms of the age and gender composition of the dwelling unit; the interviewer might be instructed to survey the oldest male or the second oldest female, for example. Note that this information about the characteristics of individuals within the household does not have to be known earlier in the sampling process; indeed, this kind of sampling scheme requires no prior knowledge about individuals, which can be difficult to acquire, but only knowledge about geographical entities, which is easily obtained.

Sampling techniques for telephone interviewing

The preceding sampling designs are the classic ones covered in most texts on survey research. However, they do not include the dominant technique used by major polling organizations conducting telephone interviews. Telephone surveys are the most prominent kind of survey to measure public opinion for a number of reasons. The first is speed. Often pollsters want to assess as quickly as possible the public's reaction to a major event, such as the United States' bombing of Libya in 1986 or the destruction of the space shuttle *Challenger* the same year; personal interviews and mailed questionnaires take too much time. Moreover, telephone interviews are substantially cheaper than personal interviews, yet they still enable the interviewer to collect detailed and pertinent information from the respondent. Although respondents tend to become fatigued much more quickly in a telephone interview than in a personal interview, there usually is enough time to conduct a reasonably extensive interview. The telephone also has the virtue in many instances of being less threatening and intrusive; one does not have to let a stranger in one's home in order to participate in the interview.

At one time telephone-based samples were suspect because of the obvious class bias in the use of telephones; poor families were less likely to have phones. Today home phones are almost universal, which makes phone samples more appropriate even though some class bias still exists. In earlier years the telephone book was used as the basis from which to pick a sample. Although the phone book is still used today, particularly for local samples, it has a number of problems. One is that the phone book is always out of date because of the mobility of the U.S. population; the older the book, the worse the problem. Moreover, picking a national sample from the phone book would be a logistical nightmare since there are almost 5,000 phone books that would need to be referenced. But the most serious problem with the phone book is unlisted telephone numbers; in some areas the percentage of unlisted numbers is 30 percent or higher.

One way around the problems inherent in the phone book is a technique called *random-digit dialing*. Random numbers are generated to produce the telephone numbers to be called. With random-digit dialing, it is critical to know which area codes and which exchanges (the first three digits in the seven-digit telephone number) are in use. Once this information is collected, a computer random-number generator or a table of random numbers can be used to provide the last four digits of the telephone numbers. This procedure does result in unlisted numbers being reached as evidenced by the surprised reactions of respondents who ask, "How did you get my number? It's unlisted!"

Sample size

Sample size is a major puzzle for Americans who wonder how a national sample of 1,500 respondents could accurately represent the views of 180 million adult Americans. Contributing to the puzzlement is the fact that an equally accurate statewide survey might require a sample of 750 to 1,000 respondents even though any particular state's population is only a small proportion of the national total. The few cases required for a good sample and the weak relationship between the size of the sample and the size of the population from which it is drawn make many citizens who are aware of these apparent anomalies skeptical of the polling enterprise.

Statistical and probability theory explain why such small sample sizes suffice, but this is not very enlightening to the poll skeptic without an extensive mathematical background. More helpful perhaps is an analogy. To perform a blood test, for example, a medical technician draws only a drop or two of blood from the patient. This very small sample of the total amount of blood in the patient's body is sufficient since any particular drop has properties identical to the remaining blood. The technician does not need to choose the specific blood cells to be tested. Indeed, one would not want the technician to draw too large a sample of one's blood lest the blood test be more harmful than the potential ailment being investigated.

Another sample size analogy concerns the chef testing whether more spices need to be added to a large kettle of soup. The chef might sample the soup's flavor by tasting one spoonful, certainly a very small sample. Unlike in the blood analogy, however, all spoonfuls of soup may not be comparable unless the chef first carefully stirs the mixture. But if the soup is stirred properly, most readers would agree that a spoonful or two would be sufficient to determine whether more spices should be added.

Because the major cost in public opinion polling is interviewing the selected sample, it becomes critical to select a sample that suits both the purposes and the budget of the research. There is no particular virtue in large samples. Poorly selected, they provide no guarantees of accurate results. The classic example is the infamous *Literary Digest* poll of 1936 that confidently predicted a sweeping victory for Republican presidential candidate Alf Landon based upon a sample of over 2 million; Franklin Roosevelt carried forty-six of the forty-eight states in the November election. The *Literary Digest* poll failed because of unrepresentativeness of the respondents who were selected from telephone books and automobile registrations, which skewed the sample to the upper end of the socioeconomic continuum. This method of sample selection had worked well for the *Literary Digest* in previous elections, but it failed in the depression year of 1936. Many poor people without cars and phones flocked to the polls (many for the first time) to vote for Roosevelt.

One determinant of sample size is the amount of sampling error that can be tolerated in the poll. Sampling error is simply the difference

GRIN AND BEAR IT by Lichty and Wagner © 1982 Field Enterprises, Inc.
by permission of North America Syndicate, Inc.

"Ninety-nine percent of the workers at the jellybean factory think the president is doing a good job."

between the estimates obtained from the sample and the true population value. National samples of Americans typically have a sampling error of about 4 percent; this means that if the sample indicates that 52 percent of the respondents approve of the president's performance, the actual value is likely to be in the range of 48 to 56 percent (52 plus or minus 4 percent). How likely is measured by the *confidence level.* In this example a 95 percent confidence level would mean that in 95 out of 100 samples that might be selected, the sample would generate an estimate of presidential approval within the range of 48 to 56 percent.

One way to increase the confidence level and reduce the sampling error is to increase the sample size, but larger samples mean higher costs. Thus, a 4 percent sampling error normally suffices. A number of caveats, however, should be kept in mind. First, in some instances a 4 percent error will be too large given the predictions the investigator might want to make. For example, if the sample shows 51 percent planning to vote Republican with a 4 percent sampling error, then the election outcome cannot be firmly predicted since the Republican vote could be as low as 47 percent or as high as 55 percent. But if the poll indicates that 70 percent are planning to vote Republican, then a sampling error of 4 percent or higher will scarcely affect the conclusions.

Second, the sampling error of the overall sample may be only 4 percent, but the sampling error associated with estimates based on subsets of the sample can be substantially higher, particularly for numerically small groups within the sample. In subgroup analysis the original sample is subdivided into a number of mutually exclusive subsets. For example, if one were interested in comparing the political attitudes of Protestants, Catholics, and Jews based on a national sample of about 1,500 respondents, one would subdivide the sample into these three religious groups. The sampling error associated with the Jewish estimates would be much higher since there would be only forty to sixty Jewish respondents in the sample, given the distribution of Jews in the overall population. If one wished to compare across religious *and* gender groups simultaneously, then the sample would be divided into six categories: male Protestants, male Catholics, male Jews, female Protestants, female Catholics, and female Jews, and the sampling error associated with these classifications would be even larger. In general, as the original sample is subdivided into increasingly smaller subsets, the sampling error will get larger and larger.

A controversy about the level of support enjoyed by President Reagan among black Americans illustrates, among other things, the need to be sensitive to the large sampling error associated with small subsets of respondents. A CBS News/*New York Times* poll in December 1985 became a major news story (Clymer 1986a) when it "showed" that 56 percent of black respondents approved of President Reagan's performance, and only 24 percent disapproved, a level of support dramatically higher than the president had ever enjoyed. Yet an ABC News/*Washington Post* poll in January 1986 found that only 23 percent of blacks approved of the job the president was doing, and 63 percent disapproved. Which poll, if any, was more accurate? The Reagan administration preferred the positive poll, while critics of the administration believed the negative results.

In retrospect, it seems clear that the positive results in the December 1985 CBS News/*New York Times* poll were misleading and incorrect. The poll interviewed a national sample of 1,358 Americans of whom 150 were black. Thus, the sampling error for the black estimates was high, 9 percent. In contrast, the ABC News/*Washington Post* survey was of a specially designed national sample of 1,022 black Americans. With a sampling error of 3.5 percent, it was more reliable than the CBS News/*New York Times* poll. Other polls conducted at about the same time confirmed the ABC News/*Washington Post* results; a Gallup survey showed Reagan with a 23 perent approval rating among blacks, while a *Los Angeles Times* poll showed 37 percent support.

The next CBS News/*New York Times* poll done in January 1986 was in line with other polls, showing the president with 37 percent support among blacks and thereby contradicting the December CBS News/*New York Times* survey. Adam Clymer, director of polling operations at the *Times,* attributed the discrepancy between the two polls to a bad sample and sampling error:

> It now appears that our December poll had a very unrepresentative black sample, especially of black men, and the findings plainly exceeded normal sampling error. This month's sample appears, on matters from education to household size, much more representative of the black population as a whole. (Apple 1986, A-14)

Although the controversy about black support for the president was resolved, Sussman (1986a) noted that a puzzle still remained, namely that the January 1986 CBS News/*New York Times* poll showed the president with 37 percent approval, considerably higher than the 23 percent approval rating reported in the January 1986 ABC News/*Washington Post* poll. He cited three possible reasons for the difference. The first was sampling error. The ABC News/*Washington Post* poll had an error of 3.5 percent as mentioned earlier, whereas the CBS News/*New York Times* poll had an error of 7 percent since there were 189 black respondents in the total sample of 1,581. Another source of divergence was the race of the interviewers. The CBS News/*New York Times* poll employed white and black interviewers, while the ABC News/*Washington Post* poll used black interviewers only, some of whom may have "sounded black" over the telephone. This may have led black respondents to the ABC News/*Washington Post* poll to be more negative toward the president because that seemed to be the "appropriate" black response. Finally, Sussman noted that the ABC News/*Washington Post* poll began with an explicit statement that it was a survey of blacks. This may have led the respondents to take more of a black perspective and therefore be more critical of the president.

Different survey organizations provide their audiences with different amounts of information about their surveys. Most tell the date of the interviews, the method of data collection, the size of the actual sample, and the sampling error of the overall sample. For example, on April 7, 1986, *Newsweek* provided this information to its readers concerning a poll on American reactions to the bombing of Libya, which it had commissioned the Gallup Organization to conduct:

> The Gallup Organization interviewed a representative national sample of 606 adults by telephone March 26 and March 27. The margin of error is plus or minus 5 percentage points. Some "Don't know" responses were omitted.

News releases from the media vary in the amount of information they provide. For example, the CBS News/*New York Times* poll releases (in contrast to *New York Times* stories) typically include a simple and not very informative statement like this:

> This poll was conducted among a nation-wide random sample of 1,601 adults interviewed by telephone April 6-10, 1986. The error due to sampling could be plus or minus three percentage points for results based on the entire sample.

The [Newark, New Jersey] *Star-Ledger*/Eagleton Institute at Rutgers University poll provides more information including a definition of sampling error. Its background memo released March 16, 1986, warned that "sampling error does not take into account the possible sources of error inherent in any study of public opinion." The memo did not specify, however, the sources of these nonsampling errors. ABC News provides much more information about its methodology and is more explicit about the sources of error than is CBS News. For example, in its February-March 1986 release, in addition to the standard information, ABC News also explained how the telephone sample was selected, informed the reader that the survey responses were "weighted by age, sex, education and race using the latest U.S. Census figures," warned that in addition to sampling error "inaccuracy may occur from the wording of certain questions or the order in which they are asked," and presented "full results of poll questions in the order they were asked." With respect to poll information provided in actual newspaper stories, the *New York Times* and the *Washington Post* set an enviable standard of reporting (see the conclusion of Chapter 6).

Obviously, the more information that is provided about the methodology of the poll, the better one can judge the soundness of the poll results. For example, two polls conducted in Chicago in the same week in 1986 obtained sharply dissimilar results in mayoral election trial heats between incumbent mayor Harold Washington and former mayor Jane Byrne. An ABC News/WLS survey showed Washington ahead of Byrne by a margin of 58 to 35 percent, while a Northwestern University poll had Byrne ahead of Washington by 43 to 34 percent.

Paul Lavrakas analyzed the differences between the two polls and pointed out three factors that might have affected the results. The first dealt with callbacks, that is, efforts made to interview respondents who initially could not be contacted for whatever reasons. Because the Northwestern survey was conducted over three evenings, in contrast to two for the ABC News poll, and thus had more time for callbacks, the Northwestern survey may have done a better job of tracking down hard to reach respondents. A second difference was that the Northwestern survey weighted its results to reflect the demographics of Chicago's adult population. The ABC News poll did not weight its data and, according to Lavrakas, overrepresented blacks in its sample because it sought to have the black-white sample distribution reflect the 1980 census estimates of Chicago's *overall* racial composition as opposed to its *adult* racial composition. Finally, the trial heat question used by ABC News followed a question that asked respondents to choose among three candidates—Byrne, Washington, and Richard Daley, son of the former mayor. Because of hostility between Byrne and Daley supporters, it is possible that this question affected the responses to the Byrne-Washington query so that Daley supporters opted disproportionately for Washington. Although Lavrakas refused to conclude that the Northwestern poll results were likely to be more sound, his analysis does indicate how information about poll methodology can help consumers of public opinion polls sort out conflicting claims and results (Lavrakas 1986).

Total sample size vs. actual sample size

When a sample of citizens is interviewed, not every respondent answers every question. Some respondents may refuse to answer, others may have their answers screened out because they reflect nonattitudes, and still others may have no opinion on the matter. In some instances the difference between the total sample size and the actual number of people responding to or being included in the reporting of the results of a particular question can be substantial. Consider the following hypothetical situation in which 1,500 Americans are asked about their vote preferences one month before an election. Perhaps only 80 percent of the sample are registered to vote and only 60 percent of those registered will actually vote on election day. Assuming that the investigator wants to report the vote preferences of likely voters only and is able to identify that group (a difficult task), then the effective sample has shrunk from 1,500 to 720 (0.80 x 0.60 x 1,500) with an attendant increase in sampling error. And of these 720, 3 percent might refuse to reveal their preference, and another 22 percent might be unsure, thereby reducing the 720 to 540 likely voters with definite vote preferences or 36 percent of the original sample of 1,500. Of the 540 likely voters, 300 may intend to vote Democratic and 240 to vote Republican, a 56 to 44 percent split. It would be important to report this split and describe the subset of the sample from which it was calculated.

A real-life example of the importance of reporting actual sample size is provided by a July 1985 ABC News/*Washington Post* poll on the Strategic Defense Initiative ("Star Wars") (Lardner 1985). The three questions and responses were:

Q. Have you read or heard about plans by the Reagan administration to develop weapons in outer space that could destroy nuclear missiles fired at the United States by the Soviet Union or other countries? Reagan calls the research on these weapons SDI, for Strategic Defense Initiative, and some people refer to it as "Star Wars."

Yes, have read or heard	84%
No, have not read or heard	16%
Don't know or no opinion	1%

Q. Supporters say such weapons could guarantee protection of the United States from nuclear attack and are worth whatever they cost. Opponents say such weapons will not work, will increase the arms race, and the research will cost many billions of dollars. How about you: would you say you approve or disapprove of plans to develop such space-based weapons?

Approve	41%
Disapprove	53%
Don't know or no opinion	5%

Q. (For those who approved) Currently the United States and the Soviet Union have an anti-ballistic missile treaty that prohibits both nations from developing certain weapons. Suppose the U.S. had to violate or abandon that treaty in order to develop the space-based weapons. Would you still favor development of those space-based weapons or not?

Yes, would still favor	63%
No, would not still favor	32%
Don't know or no opinion	5%

Fortunately, Lardner was very careful in his reporting of the responses to the last question for, without the appropriate qualifications, one might interpret the result as showing strong support for the weapon even if the United States had to scrap the treaty. Note that the 63 percent favoring SDI represents only 26 percent (0.41 x 0.63) of the original sample of 1,506 and only 22 percent (0.41 x 0.63 x 0.84) of those respondents who had read or heard about the plans initially. It would obviously be misleading and unscrupulous to release only the results of the last item without the necessary qualifiers. Unfortunately, advocates of specific causes have at times been highly selective in their use of poll information with the conscious aim of swaying the public to their positions.

One increasingly frequent problem for pollsters is *nonresponses.* The people who have been selected for the sample either refuse to participate in the interview at all or they cannot be located and contacted for whatever reason (Stinchcombe, Jones, and Sheatsley 1981; Steen 1981). With respect to the treatment of nonresponses, the poll consumer is very much at the mercy of the polling organization. One approach by pollsters is to weight the sample according to known population characteristics obtained from the census data. This procedure assumes a similar distribution of answers among respondents and nonrespondents with similar demographic characteristics, an assumption that is sometimes faulty.

Conclusion

For many Americans, sampling is the most problematic feature of public opinion polling. Many citizens doubt whether the "small" samples reported in the media can adequately represent the population of whatever entity is being studied. Normally, citizens are at the mercy of the polling organization to select a good sample. They may question the wording of a poll, but it is very difficult for them to offer informed criticism of sampling procedures unless the polling organization provides sufficient information about such matters as the size of the sample, sampling error and confidence levels, the dates of the interviewing, and the method of interviewing. Even though sampling is considered to be statistical and scientific, sampling problems can arise that may undermine the results and interpretations of public opinion polls.

Interviewing procedures ⎯⎯ 5

Unless one has participated in a public opinion survey, it is difficult to appreciate the critical role that the interviewer plays in measuring public opinion. In general, polling organizations provide little or no information to the citizen about the interviewing process with the result that one cannot make independent judgments about the quality of the interviews and must therefore assume that they have been conducted competently. This is undoubtedly a safe assumption for the major, prestigious, and highly visible polls.

Nevertheless, as one who routinely agrees to be a respondent in public opinion, market research, and academic research surveys, I have been surprised by the obvious disparities in the training and competence of the interviewers. Often I will ask the interviewer what a certain question means or complain about the range of alternatives available to me. Some interviewers are well trained to handle such reactions, but others obviously are not. One interviewer agreed with my frustration about a particular item and informed me that there had been many complaints about the survey. Another interviewer, when I strenuously objected to the alternatives, pleaded with me to pick one of the given choices since she did not know how to handle volunteered responses. In yet another situation the interviewer told me that she would place my aberrant response in the category in which she thought it would best fit.

The purpose of this chapter is to alert the consumer of polls to the potential effects of the interviewing process on poll results. First, the methods by which the data are collected are explained; here we will discuss the advantages and disadvantages of three approaches—mailed questionnaires, telephone interviews, and personal interviews. Then we will examine the interview situation itself and a number of factors, such as sex, socioeconomic status, race, and ethnicity of the interviewer, that can affect responses.

Methods of collecting polling information _____

Mailed questionnaires

Mailed questionnaires are a very common method of assessing opinions, particularly by organizations with access to good mailing lists. As discussed in Chapter 1, interest groups frequently use mailed surveys in conjunction with their fund-raising efforts. Mailed questionnaires have a number of obvious advantages, the main one being their low cost. Because mailed surveys are self-administered by the respondent, there are no interviewers to train and support, and this dramatically reduces costs. Moreover, interviewer bias will not affect the results. And the privacy in which a mailed survey can be completed may reassure the respondent about the anonymity and confidentiality of his or her responses, thereby resulting perhaps in franker responses.

These advantages of mailed questionnaires, however, are typically outweighed by their limitations. Foremost among them are response rates that tend to be lower than those for telephone and personal interviews. This disadvantage of mailed questionnaires may have lessened over time, in part because of the higher refusal rates currently being experienced in personal and telephone interviews and because of improved techniques for generating better response rates to mailed questionnaires (Goyder 1985). A related problem with mailed surveys is the difficulty of ascertaining just how representative the respondents are of the actual population.

Much information is lost in self-administered surveys. For example, one cannot even be sure who actually completed the questionnaire, a serious limitation when surveying elite populations such as members of Congress or state legislators who are bombarded with mailed questionnaires and therefore may have a staff person fill out the survey. One also loses information about respondents' reactions to the survey and about the environment within which the survey was completed. Because there is no interviewer present to assist respondents who are having difficulty with the questionnaire, the instructions must be explicit and the questions as unambiguous as possible. There is no opportunity for clarifications.

Mailed questionnaires must not be too burdensome for the respondent or the response rate will plummet. Whenever I receive a questionnaire in the mail, I first check the number of open-ended questions that would require me to write mini-essays. If there are many, I'm likely to toss the questionnaire in the circular file unless it addresses a topic of particular interest to me. Mailed questionnaires are largely limited to highly structured, fixed alternative questions. Such items are often very annoying to citizens, particularly to political elites who complain that the political world is too complicated and their own opinions too complex to be captured in a fixed alternative item.

The burdens imposed by a mailed questionnaire are not uniform across the population. Poorly educated respondents will have more difficulty with the survey, and illiterate persons may simply have to ignore it. In addition, there is no way of knowing the order in which any particular respondent answered the questions. Certainly, some people will read the entire survey before responding, while others will start at the beginning and proceed sequentially. This means that the questionnaire may elicit different responses for individuals depending on the order in which they approached the questions. Finally, mailed questionnaires are inappropriate if the investigator needs a quick response to the topic, such as a presidential debate or foreign policy crisis. Several weeks should be allowed for the questionnaires to be returned.

Telephone interviews

Telephone interviews, on the other hand, can be done quickly (often in only two to four days and sometimes in a single evening), thereby providing an almost instantaneous reaction to a political event. Another advantage is that by using random-digit dialing techniques, a representative sample can be easily picked. Telephone interviews are less costly than personal interviews and generate a good response rate, although typically not as high as for personal interviews. In some situations telephone interviewing may succeed where no other method could because of the sensitivity of the topic or because respondents would not allow a stranger in their home to conduct a personal interview.

Telephone interviews also have shortcomings. Despite widespread possession of telephones, there is still some bias in phone interviews against respondents of low socioeconomic status who cannot afford phones. Respondents become fatigued more quickly in a telephone interview than in a personal interview, which limits how ambitious a phone survey can be (although recent experiences indicate that phone surveys can be lengthier than originally thought). Costs are incurred in training interviewers in order to avoid unwanted effects from the interviewing process. Finally, the use of the telephone eliminates the possibility of visual aids during the interview unless materials are sent to respondents in a preliminary mailing.

In the past decade a number of developments have made telephone interviews more efficient, accurate, and quick. The foremost is the advent of *computer-assisted telephone interviewing* (CATI). With CATI, the interviewing is done at video display terminals by interviewers who feed the responses directly into the computer. The overall flow and logic of the interview is controlled by a computer program. Among other things, the program makes sure that the questions are asked in the correct sequence and that the responses are consistent with the question(s) being asked (Frey 1983, 144-145). Running totals are easily generated with CATI so that results are available almost instantaneously.

Personal interviews

Personal interviews generally provide the richest and most complete information for numerous reasons. Respondents are willing to participate in lengthy personal interviews, particularly if the interviewer is skillful in developing rapport with the respondent. The response rate tends to be high and representative samples more readily selected and interviewed. The presence of the interviewer allows for an assessment of the respondent's problems with and reactions to the survey. The interviewer can directly record not only the verbal responses of the interviewee but also nonverbal behavior such as squirming, sweating, and other signs of unease with the interview situation. Moreover, the opportunity to ask follow-up questions (and to know when to probe) is greater in a personal interview than in a telephone survey.

The obvious drawbacks of personal interviews are their cost and the danger of substantial interviewer effects and biases. Costs are increased because of the need to train interviewers and to support them in the field, often with housing, meals, and transportation allowances as well as their regular salary. Because the interview is a social situation, the presence of poorly trained interviewers may alter the interpersonal dynamics of the interview and thereby influence respondents' answers in undesirable and often unpredictable ways. It is to this topic of interviewer effects and biases that we turn to next.

"I'd put that down as a definite no."

GRIN AND BEAR IT by Fred Wagner © 1984 Field Enterprises, Inc.
by permission of North America Syndicate, Inc.

Interviewer effects in public opinion polling————

For most respondents, the interview experience is a new one with all of its attendant uncertainties and ambiguities. Unsure of how to behave, respondents may look to the interview situation for appropriate cues. And certainly the two most prominent sources of cues are the survey instrument itself and the person who administers the questionnaire, the interviewer. Interviewer effects can occur in both telephone and personal interviews, although they are likely to be more pronounced in personal interviews because of the face-to-face interaction between the interviewer and the respondent. The cues provided by the survey instrument are direct (even if the questions are flawed), but the cues provided by the interviewer can be far more subtle. Moreover, if the interviewer is inconsistent in the cues given to different respondents, then the reliability of the survey results may be undermined. At the minimum, the interviewer must not change the question wording,

71

question order, or voice intonations from respondent to respondent. And since most polls use multiple interviewers, the interviewing process must be as standardized as possible, which requires careful training of interviewers.

This emphasis on consistency and uniformity in the interviewing process reflects a concern with the reliability of the measuring instrument (the questionnaire). One type of reliability measure is based on *equivalence,* the extent to which different investigators applying the same measurement instrument to the same individuals obtain consistent results. The identity of an interviewer ideally should not affect the responses that the questionnaire generates in the interview.

The reliability of an instrument can be distinguished from its *validity,* the extent to which the instrument measures what it is supposed to measure. For example, consider the second political efficacy item discussed in Chapter 3: "voting is the only way that people like me can have any say about how the government runs things." A disagree response to this item is considered an efficacious reply since it presumably means that the respondent is saying that there are ways other than voting by which he or she can be influential. But what if the individual rejects this statement because he or she believes that there is no way that people can have influence? If this is the case, then a disagree response is a sign of lack of efficacy, and the item itself is not a valid indicator of the underlying concept of political efficacy.

The interviewer's general demeanor, competence, and performance have much to do with the success of the interview. Clearly, the interviewer must be able to establish rapport with the respondent, making the respondent feel at ease and receptive to the survey. If rapport is not established, the respondent may refuse to cooperate or fail to provide complete and accurate information to the interviewer. Ideally, the interviewer is well trained about the purposes of the research and the intention of specific questions so that he or she knows whether the interviewee has fully answered the question and how to ask clarifying follow-up questions.

The interviewer certainly should not inject himself or herself into the interviewing process by making editorial comments about the respondent's replies. The interviewer should follow instructions carefully and ask all appropriate questions, yet be able to handle the unexpected events that may occur. For example, the respondent may wish to volunteer additional information. The interviewer must record and transcribe responses as accurately as possible, even when the answers do not fall neatly into one of the predetermined response categories.

"Before I tell you who I'm for, perhaps you'd be interested to hear a little something about how my political thinking has evolved over the years."

Drawing by Stevenson; ©1980 The New Yorker Magazine, Inc.

The difficulty of the interviewer's job will depend on the nature of the questionnaire as well as on the characteristics of the respondents. For example, highly structured survey items require less from the interviewer in the way of guidance and judgment, while relatively unstructured instruments require better interviewing skills. Interviews of political elites that employ open-ended questions will require the interviewer to be a good listener and prober who takes few or no notes during the interview but is able to write up the results of the interview after the formal question and answer session. Sometimes such interviews are taped, which eliminates the need to take extensive notes, but not the need to transcribe the interviews to make them more usable.

Characteristics of the interviewer, many of which cannot be changed, can affect the responses to a poll. For example, the main reason why most interviewers are middle-aged women is that this group is least threatening to male and female respondents, particularly in a personal interview in a home. Rapport is established more successfully with female interviewers. The social distance between the interviewer and the respondent can also influence the interview; if the interviewer is of obviously higher social status than the respondent, the respondent may tend to defer or acquiesce to the interviewer by providing answers that are thought to win the approval of the interviewer. Even the interviewer's manner of speech can affect the respondent's replies.

An interviewer's race and ethnicity also can affect the responses to a poll (Campbell 1981; Cotter, Cohen, and Coulter 1982; Hatchett and Schuman 1975-1976; Schuman and Converse 1971; Weeks and Moore 1981). When queried about the American political system, black respondents are more likely to give supportive, positive answers to white interviewers than to black ones. Likewise, white respondents are less likely to reveal attitudes of racial hostility when interviewed by blacks than when surveyed by whites. A January 1987 *New York Times*/WCBS-TV News poll of New Yorkers' reactions to the racial attack in Howard Beach, Queens, found that race of interviewer had a substantial effect on responses, even in telephone interviews. An earlier study by the *New York Times*/WCBS-TV News had shown that telephone respondents can correctly identify the race of the interviewer about three-fourths of the time. In the Howard Beach poll, nearly half the black respondents interviewed by whites, when asked whether the lawyer for one of the black victims had acted responsibly, thought he had not, and only about one-fourth thought the lawyer had acted responsibly. But among blacks interviewed by fellow blacks, the results were reversed (Meislin 1987).

Finally, a study by Reese et al. (1986) on the effects of interviewer ethnicity—Anglo versus Hispanic—found that ethnicity did affect the responses to certain questions. The responses of Anglos were likely to be influenced by whether the interviewers themselves were Anglo or Hispanic, especially on items that related to the culture of the interviewer. That is, when Anglos were asked questions about aspects of Mexican-American life by Hispanics, they responded more sympathetically than when asked those same questions by fellow Anglos. Why? The general explanation is that respondents try not to give answers that would offend the interviewer, particularly on matters that relate to the interviewer's race and ethnicity.

Anderson, Silver, and Abramson (1986) showed that the interviewer's race can affect behavior as well as attitudes. They examined the 1976, 1980, and 1984 National Election Studies of the Survey Research Center. These entailed pre- and postelection interviews with respondents as well as officially validated measures of whether respondents had actually voted. The investigators found that among black respondents living in northern central cities who were interviewed by blacks, 60.6 percent actually voted, compared with only 47.5 percent participation for black respondents surveyed by white interviewers. For the South, the comparable percentages were 58.1 and 45.2 percent, respectively. The preelection interview appeared "to induce changes in stated attitudes and actual behavior" (Anderson, Silver, and Abramson 1986, 15). No such race of interviewer effects could be isolated for white respondents since they were almost all surveyed by white interviewers.

Conclusion

The method of interviewing and the actual conduct of the interview measurably affect the responses to a public opinion poll. In most instances the consumer of polls is in a weak position to evaluate these effects, mainly because little information is provided about interviewing procedures. Nevertheless, there are a number of questions that the consumer might raise about the interviewing process, particularly if he or she has been selected to be a respondent in a poll. For example, if one refused to complete a mailed questionnaire, one might ask oneself why. Was it because of the subject matter, or because the questions were too simplistic, or because the questionnaire was too time consuming? If one did participate in the survey, what was one's reaction to the specifics of the questionnaire such as question wording and question order and to the overall experience itself?

Respondents to personal or telephone polls also should make some mental notes about the skill of the interviewer. How effective was the interviewer in establishing a good climate for the interview? How well did the interviewer handle one's questions and problems? Did the interviewer do anything that seemed to lead one improperly to respond in certain ways? Were there any characteristics and traits of the interviewer that either facilitated or hindered the interview? The answers to these and other questions should alert poll respondents to biases that may have influenced the interviewing process and the answers provided.

The media and the polls — 6

The media's role in public opinion polling is essentially twofold: to inform the public of poll results and to sponsor polls. The print and electronic media, especially newspapers and television, are the major sources of what Americans learn about the polls. Most citizens do not have direct access to the reports prepared by polling organizations and thus must rely on information provided by the media. Moreover, many organizations that sponsor surveys try to manipulate the media to cover poll results in ways that promote their objectives.

Some of the most publicized and widely disseminated public opinion polls are directly sponsored by the national television networks and their local affiliates, the major news magazines, and newspapers throughout the country. Thus, the media generate public opinion data that in turn become the subject matter for news stories presented by these same media. This situation has led some observers to wonder whether there might be a conflict of interest. The definition of what is newsworthy may be unduly influenced by media-sponsored polls on particular topics. In addition, the fact that the media make a substantial investment in developing their public opinion polling capability may result in a tendency to utilize that capability even when it is not appropriate to the topic at hand.

This chapter evalutes the media's reporting of public opinion polls, both polls sponsored by the media and those sponsored by other organizations. At least two distinct aspects of poll coverage are discussed: the treatment of the polls' technical features (for example, sampling error and question wording) and the presentation of the substantive results and interpretations based upon the poll data. The chapter concludes by considering the numerous problems inherent in media-sponsored polls.

Technical aspects of polls —————————————————

Various organizations have adopted standards to govern the disclosure of poll results to citizens. For example, the National Council on Public Polls (NCPP), an entity composed of polling organizations, has adopted the following Principles of Disclosure:

> All reports of survey findings of member organizations, prepared specifically for public release, will include reference to the following:
>
> —sponsorship of the survey;
> —dates of interviewing;
> —method of obtaining the interview;
> —population that was sampled;
> —size of the sample;
> —size and description of the subsample, if the survey report relies primarily on less than the total sample;
> —complete wording of questions upon which the release is based;
> —the percentages upon which conclusions are based. (Frey 1983, 189)

The recommendations go on to state:

> When survey results are released to any medium by a survey organization, the above items will be included in the release....
> Survey organizations reporting results will endeavor to have print and broadcast media include the above items in their news stories and make a report containing these items available to the public upon request. (Frey 1983, 190)

The American Association for Public Opinion Research (AAPOR) has adopted a similar set of standards with the additional recommendation that sampling error and confidence levels also be reported.

But how much protection do these standards provide the consumer of public opinion research, assuming that polling organizations follow them closely? The answer is that these standards provide less protection than is apparent at first glance, although they have contributed to improved media coverage of the polls. The standards apply primarily to survey organizations and pollsters who are releasing results rather than to the media that are covering the results, and this limits their impact. In some cases, however, the survey organization and the disseminator of the results are part of the same news organization. Coverage of in-house polls is usually more in line with the NCPP and AAPOR standards. For example, one can learn about the results of a CBS News/*New York Times* poll from four distinct sources: the story that appeared in the *New York Times*, the report that was presented on the CBS Evening News, the news release issued by the *New York Times*, and the release prepared by CBS

ENTERING

N.Y. TIMES/CBS NEWS POLL

POP. 1154

Drawing by Dana Fradon; © 1982 The New Yorker Magazine, Inc.

News. The first two sources are readily available to citizens should they choose to utilize them; the latter two are not. Normally, one can expect the news releases prepared by CBS News and by the *New York Times* and the news story that appears in the *Times* to comply closely with the NCPP and AAPOR standards; the story presented on the CBS Evening News may be less complete because of the scarcity of air time.

If the organization reporting the poll is different from the group that sponsored it, there may be major discrepancies between the poll release and the actual news story in terms of how well each meets the NCPP and AAPOR recommendations. For example, most newspapers do not conduct their own polls, but instead rely on syndicated polls from organizations such as Gallup and Harris or on news releases in the public domain that are issued by polling organizations. In these situations the NCPP recommends that the sponsoring organization should attempt to get the medium that is reporting its results to do so in conformity with the NCPP standards. But there really is no way to enforce this requirement on news organizations once the poll release has become a public document. Moreover, the interests of the sponsoring organization may not be well served by full disclosure of the technical features of the poll, particularly when the sponsoring organization has manipulated the poll to generate a desired set of results.

Another reason why the NCPP and AAPOR standards are less effective than they might be is that they do not include all of the technical aspects of a poll that can markedly affect the results. For example, the NCPP standards recommend reporting the "complete wording of questions on which the release is based." This is not necessarily identical to the complete questionnaire, but if the entire survey instrument is not provided, then it will be difficult to ascertain whether question order and placement influenced the results for those questions included in the release. For the major news organizations this is less of a concern since their overall release typically includes the entire questionnaire in the order in which the items were asked. Moreover, the television networks and major newspapers are very willing to distribute their overall poll releases to interested citizens. The more serious problem comes when a news organization prepares a news story based on a subset of items from the overall questionnaire, and the reader or viewer is not told about question wording and question order. The thrust of the news story may or may not accurately represent the content of the overall survey. Obviously, the items that are chosen for analysis and the perspective within which that analysis is placed can dramatically affect the resulting news story.

Also ignored by the NCPP and AAPOR standards are the adjustments made to the sample such as *weighting,* which might be used to achieve demographic representativeness (see Chapter 8), or *filtering,* which might be used to identify likely voters within the sample. The poll release will often state that weighting and filtering have been done, but in most cases it will not tell how. Ill-equipped to assess the soundness of the poll, the poll consumer is at the mercy of the decisions made by the analysts.

As will be discussed in Chapter 7, pollsters use different methods to identify likely voters, methods that can affect sample-based predictions in important ways. A *Denver Post* poll on the 1986 U.S. Senate race in Colorado between Democratic representative Tim Wirth and Republican representative Ken Kramer illustrates the consequences of screening for likely voters. Among the entire sample, Kramer led Wirth by 44 to 41 percent, but among "most likely" voters, Kramer was ahead by 52 to 39 percent (Rothenberg 1986c, 14). Wirth eventually won the election, which supports the politicians' cliché that the only poll that really counts is the one held on election day.

Related information omitted by the NCPP and AAPOR recommendations is the response rate and procedures, such as callbacks, that are used to increase the response rate. Poor response rates may necessitate adjustments to the interviewed sample to make it representative of the broader population. If respondents who are called back multiple times in order to complete an interview differ in systematic ways from respondents who are interviewed on the first attempt, then the decision whether to utilize multiple callbacks can affect the substantive findings of the poll. Unfortunately, in most situations the poll consumer is presented little if any information about response rates and related matters.

How closely do the media actually conform to the NCPP and AAPOR standards in their reporting of polls? Miller and Hurd (1982) conducted a study of how well three newspapers—the *Chicago Tribune,* the *Los Angeles Times,* and the *Atlanta Constitution*—followed the AAPOR guidelines. In a sample of 116 polls reported between 1972 and 1979, compliance was highest for sample size (reported 85 percent of the time) and sponsorship (reported 82 percent of the time) and lowest for sampling error (reported only 16 percent of the time). Miller and Hurd found no marked trend indicating improved poll reporting over time, but did find that compliance with the AAPOR standards on sampling error was better for election polls than for nonelection surveys. In general, newspapers did a better job of reporting their own in-house polls than on polls provided by external sources. In some instances the external polls did not provide the information called for by the AAPOR standards and therefore the newspapers could not publish it, but in other cases the newspapers simply edited out that information (Miller and Hurd 1982, 246).

Another study (Salwen 1985b) examined the reporting of public opinion polls by the *Detroit News* and the *Detroit Free Press* in presidential election years 1968 to 1984. Salwen did find improvement over time in the reporting of some of the AAPOR information, although the exact question wording and the timing of the poll were reported less frequently (about 28 and 61 percent of the time, respectively) and showed no improvement during the sixteen-year period. Reporting of sampling error did improve over time, but still in 1984 only 50 percent of the news stories about polls mentioned sampling error. Like Miller and Hurd, Salwen found that newspapers did a much better job of presenting the methodology of their in-house polls than of polls from external sources.

Miller and Hurd and Salwen are somewhat optimistic that newspaper reporting of polls has improved. They attribute improvement to an increased collaboration between journalists and social scientists, the availability of readable books and texts on polling, and the increased frequency of in-house polls (polls that newspapers do a better job of reporting because of the local interest in them and reporters' greater access to information about their technical aspects).

The guarded optimism of these studies must be tempered somewhat by the fact that they both dealt with major daily newspapers of reasonably high quality. One might expect such papers to have expertise and competence in reporting polls. Moreover, many of the polls they analyzed were election surveys, which are more likely to report information such as sample size and sampling error than are nonelection polls. However, another study by Salwen (1985a) found that with respect to question wording and method of interviewing, nonelection polls were more descriptive than were elections polls, a finding speculatively attributed to the fact that question wording and interviewing method are more self-evident in election polls and therefore need not be reported. In smaller daily and weekly newspapers without the resources to conduct in-house polls and to employ their own survey research experts, poll coverage is probably much poorer.

If newspaper reporting of polls leaves something to be desired, what must television's coverage be like? Newspapers have a number of obvious advantages in reporting polls. One is that they provide the reader with hard copy in contrast to the television message that (unless taped) "disappears" as soon as it is presented. Imagine the difference in learning about question wording from a newspaper story versus a television report. Of course, television would be less likely in the first place to present the complete question wording, in part because it typically faces more severe time and space constraints than does a daily newspaper.

Paletz et al. (1980) have conducted one of the few empirical studies of treatment of polls by network television. They examined every poll reported on the CBS and NBC evening news shows and in the *New York Times* in 1973, 1975, and 1977, years deliberately chosen to avoid presidential elections. The television networks generally did a poorer job of reporting details about polls than did the *Times*, although the latter's performance was not stellar. (Keep in mind that during the 1970s the networks and the *Times* had not yet begun extensive in-house polling; in-house polls are better reported than external surveys.) Among the findings was that the sponsor of a poll was almost never mentioned on the networks and mentioned only about 25 percent of the time in the *Times*. Sample size was presented in two-thirds of the *Times* stories, but in only 26 percent of the television reports. The time of interviewing was given in 43 percent of the *Times* accounts and in 30 percent of the television reports. And in 30 percent of the *Times* stories and only 5 percent of the television reports was the complete wording of particular questions provided. Beyond these details, technical information about the polls was virtually nonexistent (Paletz et al. 1980, 504-505).

An analysis of Australian television coverage of election polls (Smith and Verrall 1985) generally concurred with Paletz and his colleagues that television coverage was superficial and lacking in methodological details. Smith and Verrall argue that the heterogeneity of the television audience requires that coverage be kept brief and simple. One way to foster brevity and simplicity is to omit methodological information.

As the available evidence suggests, the media could do a much better job adhering to the NCPP and AAPOR standards in reporting poll results, especially for surveys that are not conducted in house. This would enable citizens to become more proficient technically in assessing and evaluating poll results. Methodological sophistication in poll reporting may gradually increase as survey research skills become more widely disseminated among journalists, political practitioners, and even the media audience. Moreover, as an increasing number of media organizations conduct their own in-house polls and ignore polls from other sources, the overall quality of poll reporting will probably improve. Nevertheless, "the way methodological information about polling is reported in the media tends more to reassure than alert the audience about the possible defects of poll data" (Paletz et al. 1980, 506).

Substantive interpretation of polls

Lacking access to the complete results of polls, citizens cannot easily evaluate how well the media report on the technical aspects of polling. It is even more problematic for them to evaluate how well the media describe and interpret the substance of public opinion polls. Because interpretation of poll data can be highly judgmental and value laden, it may be difficult to demonstrate that one particular interpretation is superior to another except in cases where obvious misreadings of the data have occurred or where blatant biases have been built into the analysis. Even simple description can pose a problem if time and space constraints force the media to cover only a subset of the items on a topic.

This section cites a number of examples to illustrate how the media use and interpret polls (a topic addressed in more detail in Chapter 8) and how much leeway the media have in deciding what parts of a poll to emphasize. The first example deals with Americans' reactions to the bombing of Libya as measured in a CBS News/*New York Times* poll conducted in April 1986. The reports of the poll in a CBS news release, in the *New York Times,* and on the CBS Evening News were very consistent, the lead being that Americans overwhelmingly approved the bombing by a margin of 77 to 14 percent, even as a plurality of 43 percent thought it would lead to more terrorism while only 30 percent thought it would reduce terrorism. The *Times* story was, of course, far more detailed about the poll's results than was the CBS Evening News presentation, but the overall consistency of both reports suggested a common interpretation.

In addition to asking citizens whether they thought the Libyan bombing would reduce or increase terrorism, respondents were asked a related item about the efficacy of American military action in general: "If the United States made it a policy to take military action against a government it believes has trained or financed terrorists, do you think that would reduce terrorism in the long run, or would it only make things worse?" Fully 57 percent said it would reduce terrorism, and only 27 percent thought it would make it worse. In the treatment of this item, the *Times* story and the CBS press release differed. The *Times* reported this question at the very end of an article that ran forty-four column inches, while in a twelve-paragraph CBS press release the item was detailed in the fourth paragraph. Neither the *Times* nor CBS News made much of the discrepancy between citizens' doubts that the Libyan bombing would reduce terrorism and their belief that a policy of taking military action against terrorist governments would reduce terrorism. But imagine the divergent portrayals of public opinion that could be painted if one or the other item had been reported, but not both. One headline could read, "Americans question effectiveness of Libyan bombing," while another proclaimed, "Americans support military response to terrorism."

A marvelous example of the choices that face the analyst is Adam Clymer's *New York Times* story on abortion attitudes based on a survey of

Americans conducted in late 1985. The wording of abortion questions has a tremendous impact on citizens' responses, a "clear indication of uncertainty and conflict" in the public's attitudes on the topic (Clymer 1986b, 22e). Three items in the survey illustrate the complexity of popular attitudes:

What do you think about abortion? Should it be legal as it is now, legal only in such cases as saving the life of the mother, rape or incest, or should it not be permitted at all?

Legal as is now	40%
Legal only to save mother, rape or incest	40
Not permitted	16
Don't know, not ascertained	4

Which of these statements comes closest to your opinion? Abortion is the same thing as murdering a child, or abortion is not murder because a fetus isn't really a person.

Murder	55%
Not murder	35
Don't know, not ascertained	10

Do you agree or disagree with the following statement? Abortion sometimes is the best course in a bad situation.

Agree	66%
Disagree	26
Don't know, not ascertained	8

Depending upon which items were emphasized and how particular items were interpreted, markedly different stories could be written. If one focused only on the first item, one could write a proabortion story that argued that 40 percent of Americans favored the current abortion policy, another 40 percent favored legalized abortion in more limited circumstances, and only 16 percent opposed abortion outright. An antiabortion story could stress that 56 percent of the sample (40 plus 16 percent) favored limiting somewhat the current availability of abortion. The second item could be used to document an antiabortion story that emphasized that a majority of Americans thought abortion was murder. But a story based only on the third item would suggest that a strong majority of Americans think abortion is sometimes the best course of action. Clymer's story reflected the complex and even contradictory nature of popular attitudes on abortion; imagine the advocacy piece that could have been written if he had adopted a blatant proabortion or antiabortion perspective.

Stories that include polling data in the *New York Times*, the

Washington Post, and other major newspapers usually integrate the polling information into the articles, often presenting detailed break-downs of the data and a reasonable amount of information about the poll and its characteristics. Newspapers not only use polls to supplement a news story, but they also have articles that are primarily based on polls. In contrast, news magazines such as *Time* and *Newsweek* often commission polls to use as appendages to a news story. Sometimes the poll results are placed in an inset with little reference made to them in the accompanying story. For example, a two-page story about the move to repeal the Twenty-second Amendment appeared in the September 8, 1986, issue of *Newsweek*, which also commissioned a poll on the subject. No mention of the poll occurred until the last paragraph of the story and the total reference to it was brief: "Reagan's approval rating in the last *Newsweek* poll is a smashing 64 percent—although the same poll shows that 62 percent oppose a third term for this president and 60 percent op-pose the repeal of the 22nd Amendment" (Morganthau 1986, 17). *Newsweek* also included an inset in its article (see box).

Note the scant analysis of the poll. There are no breakdowns by subgroups. Nowhere is it made explicitly clear whether there has been any filtering or screening done of those people who have not heard or read about the proposal. After some major political event or develop-ment, news organizations regularly sponsor polls to assess popular

---

A Newsweek Poll: Strong Opposition

Despite Reagan's immense popularity, voters do not want him to have a third term.

Have you heard or read about the pro-posal to repeal the 22nd Amendment to the Constitution to enable a president to serve more than two four-year terms?	**If the 22nd Amendment were repealed within the next two years, would it permit Ronald Reagan to run for a third term?**
61% Yes	**37%** Permit a third term for Reagan
37% No	**43%** Apply only to future presidents
Would you favor or oppose such a proposal?	**Would you like to see Ronald Reagan elected to a third term, or not?**
37% Favor	**32%** Yes
60% Oppose	**62%** No

For this NEWSWEEK Poll, The Gallup Organization interviewed a national sample of 771 adults by telephone on Aug. 20 and 21. The margin of error is plus or minus 4 percentage points. The NEWSWEEK Poll © 1986 by NEWSWEEK, Inc.

---

reactions. For example, after a House-Senate conference committee agreed upon a compromise tax reform proposal in August 1986, most of the major news organizations either conducted or commissioned a poll measuring citizens' attitudes toward tax reform. A *Newsweek* poll included the following items (September 1, 1986):

Do you approve or disapprove of the new tax bill approved by a House-Senate conference committee?

Approve very strongly	16%
Approve not so strongly	24
Disapprove very strongly	17
Disapprove not so strongly	17
Undecided	26

Do you think the new tax bill would make for a fairer distribution of the tax load among all taxpayers?

Fairer	33%
Not much different	30
Not as fair	24
No opinion	13

Do you think the new tax bill will benefit the nation's economy generally, hurt the nation's economy or not have much effect?

Benefit	27%
Hurt	20
Not much effect	41

These items are typical of the tax reform questions asked by other organizations. They scarcely recognize the problem of nonattitudes and low informational levels on this topic. Instead, respondents' answers are treated as if they reflected genuine attitudes. The epitome of silliness on this issue was reached when the following question was asked in an August 1986 Harris survey reported in the *National Journal* (September 13, 1986):

Do you favor or oppose Congress passing a tax reform bill that will cut individual taxes by $105 billion over five years, will increase business taxes by the same amount, will reduce the tax rates that most people pay, will cut the maximum tax rate for both individuals and corporations and will increase the minimum tax that wealthy individuals and corporations pay?

Favor	77%
Oppose	17

This is such a complex and multifacted question that it is not clear what citizens are responding to when they answer "favor" or "oppose." The

Harris poll also queried citizens on provisions of the tax reform proposal such as the minimum tax that wealthy individuals and corporations would have to pay, the investment tax credit for corporations, and the special deduction for two wage earners in the same family. It would have been informative to know first whether citizens actually knew what these provisions were. Undoubtedly, the amount of information possessed by citizens on some of these topics was limited, with the result that many of the responses reflected nonattitudes rather than genuine views.

The previous examples have suggested some of the problems that can be encountered in interpreting poll results. Often, however, the media do not actually interpret poll results, but instead present simple, straightforward descriptive statements. Sometimes poll data are integrated into a news story that may or may not present and utilize the data appropriately. In some cases there is in-depth substantive analysis of the poll and its implications. An excellent example of this is a February 25, 1986, *New York Times* story on the farm crisis by William Robbins that effectively incorporated polling data from a February survey conducted by CBS News/*New York Times*. Robbins reported Americans' replies to questions such as "How many farmers are facing serious economic problems today?" and "What do you think will happen to food prices if more small farmers lose their farms?" He also pointed out where agricultural economists disagreed with popular sentiments. In addition, Robbins highlighted counterintuitive features of the poll such as the fact that urban dwellers were less likely to assign blame to the farmers for their predicament than were rural residents. Throughout the news story Robbins included information about federal farm policies and linked it to citizens' attitudes where appropriate.

With respect to the statistical presentation of polling data, the most common form is simple percentage distributions for individual questions. Often there will be a breakdown by demographic subgroups such as men and women or blacks and whites, although seldom will a contingency table be presented. Measures of association, correlation analysis, and multivariate statistical analyses are virtually nonexistent, probably out of fear of intimidating and turning off the audience. The positive side of this is that the statistical procedures used in poll reporting are likely to be understood by most of the adult population. A fair summary statement is that media reporting of polls is reasonably accurate as far as it goes, in part because poll coverage is not very ambitious given the media's perception of what their audience wants and is able to comprehend.

Media, polls, and the news reporting emphasis ___

There has been much criticism of the media for promoting the polls to such a position of prominence that they become regular topics for news stories. Indeed, some observers complain that the media in their role as sponsors of polls have gone into the business of *creating* the news rather than simply *reporting* it. More and more media have developed their own polling capabilities, and in order to justify this sizable expenditure they may increasingly report poll-based stories that are not newsworthy in the traditional sense. Consider this hypothetical example. A news organization conducts a poll on American attitudes toward mass transportation when this topic is not on the national agenda and not a focal point for public debate, then publishes a story reporting the results of this survey. This story comes very close to being news that is created by the media rather than news that is coverage of real events. The media come close to generating news in their constant reporting of presidential popularity polls; the latest blip in the trend line of presidential popularity becomes a topic for a news story.

Another concern is that as more news organizations develop their own polling capabilities, they will increasingly fail to cover polls conducted by their rivals. Obviously, most of the media pollsters query citizens on matters such as presidential election trials heats, but usually their news reports do not mention the competition's results, particularly when they are discrepant with their own. One can envisage situations in which the media might explicitly choose to play an agenda-setting role by conducting a poll on an issue not yet in the public limelight and then trumpeting the results of that poll until some public official seized the issue as his or her own.

The media's treatment of election polls has received unusually harsh criticism. The most common complaint is that the media treat elections as sporting events, usually horse races (see Chapter 7), and use the polls to help handicap the outcome. Campaign coverage by the media frequently emphasizes candidates' stances on the issues less than their relative electoral standing, often as measured by the polls (Broh 1980; Asher 1984). As Robinson and Sheehan (1983, 252) argue:

> The main problem with polling ... is that it is objective and so "newsworthy" (at least for the moment) that it drives out all other forms of news. Polls have a higher priority in the newscast than most other forms of campaign reporting. And, of course, polls tend to be among the least substantive kinds of political journalism.

89

A number of observers have pointed out problems inherent in media-sponsored public opinion polling that reflect structural features of the polling and news reporting enterprises. Ladd (1980, 576) questions whether polling and journalism can fit together well given that *newsworthiness* for the media is characterized by speed and timeliness, whereas good polling, despite the current technology for quick assessments of public attitudes, requires "extensive, time-consuming explanation and exposition." This potential conflict is exacerbated by the space and time constraints faced by news organizations. Consequently, the media are often unable to present a poll-based story that includes complete details about the poll itself as well as adequate substantive background and context. Ladd also argues that good reporting is often characterized by a sharp focus and relatively unambiguous conclusions; good survey research, however, often reveals uncertainty, ambiguity, and low levels of public information and interest on matters of public policy. Often the portrait of public attitudes revealed by polls is a complex, contradictory one that may not make a "good" news story.

Crespi (1980, 473) argues that journalistic requirements affect polling in both positive and negative ways:

Positive	Negative
1. Journalistic requirements place a high value on factual documentation of poll results, in the form of actual percentages rather than fuzzy generalizations.	There is a preoccupation with reporting numbers, the "objective" poll results, with a corresponding lack of interest in their underlying meaning or patterning.
2. Subjective editorializing is devalued insofar as poll reports are concerned, reducing the likelihood that the personal views of pollsters will introduce bias.	Superficiality and lack of analysis too often characterize coverage of even the most complicated issues.
3. Attention is focused on opinion regarding specific events and issues, thereby making poll results relevant to the real-life experiences and problems of the public, and to the political process.	Topics that can be expected to create front-page headlines dominate, leading to a spasmodic coverage of the agenda of public concerns.
4. Sensitivity to changes in public opinion, resulting from the effects of events, is enhanced.	There is limited continuing coverage of long-term trends, and background news is often neglected.

Conclusion

Although one need not agree entirely with Crespi, it is clear that the polling-media relationship can be difficult and complex. If poll sponsors recognize both the uses and limitations of polls, the relationship also can be very beneficial and informative to citizens. After all, the ability to ascertain public opinion in a timely and accurate fashion on matters of civic importance is an amazing accomplishment. But pollsters and the media need to provide their audiences with sufficient information about how the poll was conducted so that informed judgments can be made. Reporting sample size and sampling error is the beginning of good poll coverage by the media and not the end. Information must also be presented about question wording and question order, factors that can have a much greater effect on the responses than can sampling error.

The *New York Times* and the *Washington Post* usually do a good job of informing their readers about the technical features of their surveys. An April 17, 1986, *Times* story included the following description of the poll on page nine:

> The latest *New York Times*/CBS News Poll is based on telephone interviews conducted on April 15 with 704 adults across the United States, excluding Alaska and Hawaii.
>
> The sample of telephone exchanges called was selected by a computer from a complete list of exchanges in the country. The exchanges were chosen so as to insure that each region of the country was represented in proportion to its population. For each exchange, the telephone numbers were formed by random digits, thus permitting access to both listed and unlisted numbers.
>
> The results have been weighted to take account of household size and number of residential telephones and to adjust for variations in the sample relating to region, race, sex, age and education.
>
> In theory, in 19 cases out of 20 the results based on such samples will differ by no more than 4 percentage points in either direction from what would have been obtained by interviewing all adult Americans. The error for smaller subgroups is larger. For example, the potential error for men is plus or minus 6 percentage points, and for women it is plus or minus 5 percentage points.
>
> In addition to sampling error, the practical difficulties of conducting any survey of public opinion may introduce other sources of error into the poll.

Note that in addition to the standard information, the *Times* briefly described random-digit dialing, explicitly stated that the data had been weighted, and discussed sampling error for subgroups. The last sentence of the statement mentioned other sources of error, but unfortunately did

not provide examples of them or elaborate on their potential consequences. Despite this major omission, the *Times* description of its polls is
one of the best available. Even more important than describing the
technical details of polls, the media should conscientiously ensure that
the substance of their stories accurately reflects the polling data.

Polls and elections 7

The type of polling most likely to be familiar to Americans is election surveys. Along with surveys about presidential performance, they receive substantial and continuing coverage in the media and generate the most controversy, particularly when preelection polls incorrectly predict the election day outcome. Although the most prominent election polls focus on the presidential contest, the use of polls has expanded to almost all congressional contests as well as to many state and local races.

Sponsors of election polls

Among the many sponsors of election polls are candidates or political parties. They use polls as research tools to collect information in order to devise and implement a winning campaign strategy. Typically, candidate-sponsored polls obtain information from citizens about their perceptions of the candidates, their views on the issues, and their own sociodemographic characteristics. Polls are used to assess the relative strengths and weaknesses of the candidates with respect to their personal attributes as well as their issue stances. Polls enable candidates to determine how well they are running overall, how their campaigns are going within electorally important subgroups, and how campaign events and media advertising have affected their standing among the voters.

A second major source of election polls is the mass media. Polls are a central focus of their election coverage. Indeed, the media have been criticized (Asher 1984, 234-247) for treating elections as if they were horse races, emphasizing not what the candidates say on the issues, but their relative standing in the polls: "Who's ahead?" "Who's behind?"

"Who's gaining?" and "Who's falling back in the pack?" Of course, media polls go beyond simply recording levels of support for the candidates. Often they address topics such as patterns of support for the candidates among groups of voters defined by their demographic characteristics and issue stances.

The distinction between candidate and media polls often becomes blurred, particularly when candidates try to manipulate the media so that the results of both kinds of polls show the candidates in the best possible light or at least minimize the damage caused by an adverse poll result. It is not uncommon for candidates to selectively leak their own polls in hopes of getting a helpful story in the media. Likewise, candidates may criticize the accuracy of media-sponsored polls to minimize their negative effects.

This chapter describes various types and uses of polls that are common to election campaigns. Candidates and parties often attempt to use polls for purposes other than research and to manipulate media coverage of them. The role of polling during the presidential primary season and general election and how and why polls can go wrong in making election predictions are also discussed. The chapter concludes with a speculative analysis of how polls may affect the way citizens vote.

Types of election polls

The differences among the many kinds of election polls are less methodological and more a function of the purposes for which they have been conducted. Some of the candidate- and party-sponsored polls such as tracking surveys may remain private tools of the campaign; media-generated surveys such as exit polls often become topics of major public controversy. It is important for the consumer of public opinion polls to be aware of the different kinds of surveys and what they can tell us about elections.

Benchmark survey

A benchmark survey is usually conducted after a candidate has decided to seek office. Designed to provide a base line from which to evaluate the subsequent progress of the campaign, a benchmark survey collects standard information about the public image of candidates, their positions on issues, and the demographics of the electorate. Three important pieces of information often gathered in a benchmark survey are the candidates' name recognition levels, their electoral strength vis-à-vis their opponents', and citizens' evaluations of the performance of the incumbent officeholder.

One problem with a benchmark survey is its timing. The earlier it is done, the less likely the respondent will know anything about the challenger and the more likely that the political and economic situation might change dramatically by the time the election nears. Nevertheless, useful information can still be collected about voters' perceptions of the strengths and weaknesses of the incumbent, their perceptions of the ideal candidate, and their views on major policy issues. The results of a benchmark survey normally are not publicized or leaked unless they show the candidate doing surprisingly well.

Trial heat survey

Technically, a trial heat survey is not a survey but a question or series of questions within a survey. Media stories abound about the results of trial heat questions, especially on presidential contests, so it is worthwhile to devote special attention to this enterprise.

Trial heat questions group candidates together in hypothetical matchups and ask citizens for whom they would vote in that hypothetical pairing. For example, a May 1986 ABC News/*Washington Post* poll asked a sample of Americans their preferences for the 1988 Republican and Democratic presidential nominations and their preferences between pairs of Democratic and Republican nominees (Sussman 1986d, 14). Potential Republican primary voters, when asked to choose from a list of seven possible nominees, gave George Bush, the vice president, a big advantage with 58 percent of the vote; Howard Baker, the former Senate majority leader, a distant second with 14 percent; Robert Dole, the Senate majority leader at the time, 12 percent; and Paul Laxalt, a U.S. senator, 2 percent. From a list of nine names on the Democratic side, 33 percent of potential Democratic voters selected U.S. Senator Gary Hart, 19 percent Chrysler chairman Lee Iacocca, 18 percent the Reverend Jesse Jackson, and 16 percent New York governor Mario Cuomo. Trailing the field was U.S. Senator Joseph Biden of Delaware with 1 percent and Arizona governor Bruce Babbitt with less than 0.5 percent. In the trial heat between Bush and Hart, Hart had a narrow 47 to 46 percent lead among all respondents and a 48 to 45 percent lead among registered voters; in every other trial heat pairing Bush with other potential Democratic nominees, Bush enjoyed a modest to substantial lead.

Trial heat questions are fun, the grist for interesting political gossip and speculation. But a number of caveats must be kept in mind. Typically, a trial heat question is phrased, "If the election were held today, would you vote for. . . ?" The point, of course, is that the election is not being held today. The election may be a year or two away, and in that period much can happen to alter the standing of the candidates. Trial heat questions far in advance of an election measure name recognition more than anything else. It is not surprising that Bush and Hart topped the above-mentioned poll and that Laxalt, Biden, and Babbitt trailed badly.

One must be careful not to view trial heat placements as immutable, nor should one be surprised when the standing of the candidates changes dramatically. Another factor to consider in a trial heat question is whether the political party affiliation of the candidate is given. With well-known candidates such as Bush and Hart, it makes little difference whether party affiliation is mentioned, but in less prestigious races between lesser known candidates, it can make a substantial difference if the question is phrased "John Doe versus Joe Blitz" or "John Doe, the Democrat, versus Joe Blitz, the Republican."

Tracking polls

Tracking polls are done by a campaign, most often on a daily basis near election day, to monitor closely any late shifts in support. Tracking polls are a tremendous resource for a candidate for they provide the most up-to-date information on which to base any last-minute shifts in campaign strategy and media advertising. Because tracking polls are expensive, they rely upon *rolling samples.* For example, samples of size 100 may be collected on four consecutive days. Although an N of 100 is small and has a large sampling error, an N of 400 is much more reliable. But much can happen between the first and fourth day of interviewing, perhaps making the oldest interviews less interesting to the campaign. Hence, on the fifth day another 100 people would be interviewed and added to the sample and the first 100 responses discarded. And on the sixth day, another 100 people would be interviewed, while the 100 interviews done on the second day would be eliminated. This procedure guarantees an overall sample of 400 that includes 100 new interviews each day, thereby allowing a close and timely monitoring of voters' reactions to the campaign. One danger of tracking polls is that any single day's interviews could be highly aberrant; the candidate and campaign must be careful not to overreact to what might be only a statistical blip.

One of the best examples of the value of tracking polls occurred in 1982 in the Missouri Senate race in which incumbent Republican U.S. senator John Danforth was challenged by Democratic state senator Harriet Woods (Newman 1983). Danforth was the strong favorite to win, but the Woods campaign caught fire toward the end, creating an extremely close contest. The Danforth campaign had ample resources to conduct tracking polls that provided valuable information about Woods's surge and enabled the campaign to respond effectively with new television ads. Danforth ultimately won the election by 27,500 votes out of 1.5 million cast. Broder (1982, 1) pointed out that in 1982 the Republican Senatorial Campaign Committee spent more than a half million dollars on tracking polls in U.S. Senate races that were expected to be close or in which polls indicated a narrowing race.

Cross-sectional vs. panel surveys

When the major polling organizations conduct multiple polls over time on an election contest, they generally employ a cross-sectional design in which different samples of citizens are selected for each round of interviewing. For example, in the 1984 presidential contest CBS News/ *New York Times* polled a telephone sample of 1,546 adult Americans between September 12 and 16 about their presidential choice. Among the probable electorate Reagan-Bush led Mondale-Ferraro 57 to 35 percent with 7 percent expressing no opinion and 1 percent volunteering that they would not vote. A few weeks later, from September 30 to October 4, CBS News/*New York Times* conducted another poll, this time of 1,229 registered adults; Reagan-Bush led Mondale-Ferraro among the probable electorate by 59 to 33 percent with 8 percent undecided.

Each of these surveys provides a picture of where the electorate stood at a single point in time, and each is based on a different sample. In comparing the results of the two surveys, we can say that the Reagan lead went from 22 to 26 percent (subject to sampling error) and that the *net* gain for Reagan was 4 percent. But we cannot tell what pattern of movement produced this net gain. Perhaps 2 percent moved from Mondale to Reagan, or 10 percent moved from Reagan to Mondale and 12 percent from Mondale to Reagan, or 30 percent moved from Reagan to Mondale and 32 percent from Mondale to Reagan. All of these hypothetical scenarios yield a net gain of 4 percent. But the total percentage of citizens who changed their preferences varies dramatically—2 percent in the first instance, 22 percent (10 plus 12 percent) in the second, and 62 percent (30 plus 32 percent) in the third.

Unfortunately, cross-sectional surveys tell us only the net amount of change that has occurred; they cannot tell us about the gross amount of change or about the pattern of individual changes that produced the net result. If one is interested simply in net changes in the relative standing of the candidates, then cross-sectional surveys are fine. But if the total volatility of voters' attitudes and preferences is the key concern, then a *panel design* is needed.

The key characteristic of a panel design is that the same individuals are interviewed two or more times. This makes panel surveys more costly and difficult since the same respondents must be located repeatedly, no easy task in light of the mobility and mortality of respondents. For example, panel surveys of college students conducted over a period of months or years can be very burdensome because of the high mobility of that age group. Another problem is that respondents may not be willing to participate in multiple interviews; moreover, respondents who do agree to be reinterviewed may differ systematically from those who do not. A final problem with panel surveys is that the experience of being interviewed at one point in time may affect the respondent's answers at the next interview. Despite these difficulties, panel surveys provide better information about the dynamics of the campaign and of voter decision making than do cross-sectional surveys.

Focus groups

Focus groups technically are not polls but in-depth interviews with a small number of people (usually ten to twenty) who often are selected to represent broad demographic groups. Focus groups might be asked to watch a candidate debate and offer reactions to it, thereby helping the candidate to prepare better for the next debate. Or the group might be shown a political commercial and be asked to react to it, thereby giving the campaign managers some insight into how effective the commercial is before actually spending money to air it. Focus group discussions are also very useful in raising and developing questions that could later be incorporated in a public opinion poll. Focus groups can be an important campaign tool even though the voter may never have heard of them.

Exit polls

Exit polls, as mentioned in Chapter 1, are interviews with voters as they are leaving polling places. These very visible and controversial polls typically ask voters for whom they voted and also collect some information on the issue positions and demographic characteristics of the respondents. The most prominent exit polls are conducted by the major news organizations to predict and explain presidential election outcomes as well as the results of congressional and major state-level races.

Exit polls have a number of advantages and uses. First, they are polls of actual voters and thus circumvent the enduring problem faced by preelection surveys of determining who actually will vote. Second, exit poll samples are collected in many states. This allows state-by-state analysis of the presidential election, an endeavor not feasible with national surveys of 1,500 respondents that are not amenable to breakdowns by state. (For details on how exit poll samples are selected, see Levy 1983.) Third, exit polls are quickly tabulated. Almost instantaneous predictions and descriptions of election outcomes are possible. Indeed, this advantage has become a central selling point for exit polls as the networks compete with each other to be the first to call an election. Finally, exit polls generate rich information that enables both journalists and social scientists to understand better the factors that helped shape the voters' choices.

The 1980 fiasco. Exit polls created a storm of controversy on election night in 1980. Although the national preelection polls had indicated a close race between Jimmy Carter and Ronald Reagan, as the results came in from the eastern time zone, it became evident that a Reagan landslide (especially in the Electoral College) was developing. What troubled many observers was that within minutes after the polls closed in a state, the networks would declare on the basis of exit polls (and not official election returns) that Reagan had carried that state. By 8:30 p.m. eastern standard time (EST), it was clear from exit poll results that Reagan had won enough states to ensure his election, no matter what happened in those states West of the Mississippi where the polls were still open (strong Reagan states in any event). Hence, the networks declared Reagan the victor while parts of the country were still voting. Moreover, Carter conceded the election before all of the polls had closed. Understandably, many concerns were raised about the effects of media declarations of victory when some voters had not yet cast their ballots. There were numerous anecdotal stories about voters in line at the polling booth leaving when they heard that the presidential race was already decided and other citizens who decided not to venture to the polls at all. In 1984 Mondale wisely waited until the polls were closed on the West Coast before conceding.

Did the early call of the 1980 presidential election actually deter citizens from voting? The empirical evidence is mixed. Works by Jackson and McGee (1981) and Jackson (1983), based upon a January 1981 reinterview of respondents who had been part of a national election sample months earlier, claimed that a combination of factors, including the early projections based on exit polls and Carter's early concession, reduced overall turnout by 6 to 12 percent. Epstein and Strom (1984), using different analysis procedures, challenged these findings, claiming that only four of forty-five respondents in the survey who decided on election day not to vote attributed their decision to their knowledge that Carter had lost. These four respondents represented only 1 percent of the total number of registered nonvoters in the sample ($N = 395$). Had they voted, the overall turnout would have increased by only 0.2 percent. Based upon official election returns from congressional districts, research by Michael X. Delli Carpini (1984) found that the early call of the 1980 election did depress turnout in both the presidential and congressional contests to the detriment of Democratic candidates. He argued that there were between five and fourteen congressional contests in which the Republican margin of victory was less than the advantage provided the GOP by the early reporting of the presidential outcome. Critical of all of the empirical studies of the effects of early reporting in 1980, Sudman (1986) concluded that congressional district turnout was depressed by 1 to 5 percent.

The early projections had no significant impact on the outcome of the presidential race in 1980, but turnout effects, no matter how small, could have been much more consequential in state and local contests. In these elections fewer votes are cast, and the margin between victory and defeat is sometimes very small. Moreover, there is the issue of projecting election results for a state before that state's polls are closed. Although there is some dispute (Busch and Lieske 1985) about how late in the day exit polls must be taken in order to obtain a representative sample and make accurate projections, it is clear that if the polls close in a state at 7:30 p.m., exit polls could in most cases accurately predict the winner by late afternoon. Widespread reporting of such projections by the media could measurably depress turnout within the state. The television networks claim that they are very careful not to make projections in a state until after the polls in that state have closed, but a 1983 study by the League of Women Voters and the Committee for the Study of the American Electorate pointed to numerous instances in which 1982 election projections were broadcast while the polls were still open. Sometimes while the polls are open the networks subtly describe the voting trends revealed by the exit polls, but do not declare a winner.

Public reaction. The opposition to exit polls has been fierce in many circles. Newspaper columnist Mike Royko urged readers to lie to exit poll interviewers, thereby undermining the usefulness of the entire enterprise. Some pollsters have been critical of exit polls and early projections. Although Roper (1985) and others believe that exit polls have few if any effects on elections, they argue that their use should be curtailed since most citizens believe that exit polls can influence election outcomes. Exit polls, they claim, undermine citizens' confidence in the electoral process and increase popular suspicion of the mass media.

Congress and state governments have sharply criticized exit polls. The U.S. House Task Force on Elections conducted hearings in 1985 critical of the news industry's use of exit polls and called for voluntary restraint on the part of the media (Swift 1985). The state of Washington went further. Recognizing that it would be difficult to prohibit the reporting of election projections and results, Washington passed a law making it a misdemeanor to do any exit interviews within 300 feet of the polls (Abrams 1985). The obvious intention of this law was to make the collection of exit data far more difficult. The law was ultimately invalidated in federal court.

The controversy surrounding exit polls remains and will likely heat up every two years. The networks argue strenuously that governmentally imposed limitations on the reporting of exit polls would be a form of censorship and a violation of First Amendment rights. The news organizations note that if the polls were open simultaneously for twenty-four hours in all fifty states, the problem of early projections would be resolved. State officials reject this option as too expensive and point out that the networks could still make premature projections for whichever states they had sufficient information. Broder (1984) has proposed a Canadian solution: have the networks come on the air by time zone from East to West, beginning each regional broadcast just as polls in that region are closing. Thus, the networks might come on in the East at 8:00 p.m. EST, in the Midwest at 9:00 p.m. EST, in the Mountain States at 10:00 p.m. EST, and on the Pacific Coast at 11:00 p.m. EST.

Consumer guidelines. The consumer of exit polls should carefully evaluate the news reports throughout election day. Any news about patterns of vote choices among various groups is most likely based upon the exit polls completed to that point. Ask yourself whether such reports might affect your likelihood of voting and your actual vote choice. Also note the time of announcement of any election projections; if the projection is made before the polls have closed, then it is based on

101

BLOOM COUNTY   by Berke Breathed

© 1984, Washington Post Writers Group, reprinted with permission.

exit polls and not official election returns since the latter are not available until after the polls close. Observe whether the projection is for a state contest or a national race; if the latter, note whether the polls are still open in some states. Finally, try to keep a mental list of the number of early projections that subsequently are contradicted by the actual vote totals.

It is unlikely that exit polls will ever be regulated except by the self-policing of the networks themselves. Exit polls are innovative and enable the news media to try to scoop their competition by being the first to call an election. The news media have heavily invested in the technology of polling and election coverage; the ability to beat the competition and to improve ratings are major payoffs for the networks on their investment.

Uses of polls by candidates _____

Candidates use polls to test the political waters in a variety of ways. For example, the prospective candidate might commission a private poll and examine public polls to assess his or her chances. Bad poll news may lead to a decision not to seek office. One reason given for Geraldine Ferraro's decision not to run for the U.S. Senate in 1986 against incumbent Republican senator Alphonse D'Amato was poll results showing her trailing substantially. Likewise, California Republican state senator Milton Marks was encouraged to challenge incumbent U.S. representative Phil Burton in 1982 by the National Republican Campaign Committee; a Wirthlin poll commissioned by the committee showed Marks leading Burton by 7 percent in February (Rothenberg

1982, 2). Marks ultimately lost. A party organization with the financial resources to conduct polls and to provide other election services may use this capability to recruit candidates. At the national level the Republican party is much better able than the Democrats to offer such assistance to its candidates and would-be candidates because of its more successful fund-raising operations based upon computerized direct mail.

Sometimes candidates will use positive poll results to generate campaign contributions or to deter contributions to their opponents. For example, in 1985 Idaho Democratic governor John Evans sent results of a poll he conducted to many political action committees (PACs) and potential contributors. The poll showed Evans in a virtual tie with incumbent Republican Steve Symms in a trial heat for the U.S. Senate seat to be voted on in 1986. Evans's action was clearly a signal to contributors that he had a good chance of being the next U.S. senator from Idaho and therefore was worthy of their donations (Rothenberg 1985, 11). Evans ultimately lost by a narrow margin.

Often when published polls show a candidate running poorly, the candidate will try to minimize the potential damage to fund raising and volunteers' morale by attacking the credibility and relevance of the poll. "The only poll that counts is the poll taken on election day," the candidate might argue and then cite examples of how the polls have been wrong in the past. Mondale's reactions to bad poll news in 1984 perfectly illustrate this response.

Sometimes the attack on the poll becomes more methodological. For example, the campaign of Jon Kyl, a candidate for the Republican nomination to the U.S. House in Arizona's Fourth Congressional District, conducted polls showing Kyl gaining strongly on frontrunner John Conlan with a third candidate, Mark Dioguardi, running far behind. Dioguardi challenged the validity of the poll, claiming that before the trial heat question that referred to all three candidates, respondents were asked a series of items that referred only to Kyl and Conlan, thereby giving respondents the misleading impression that the primary was actually a two-man race (Rothenberg 1986a, 3).

Likewise, a newspaper poll in Columbia, Missouri, showed Carrie Franche leading her chief opponent Ralph Uthlaut for the Republican nomination in the Ninth Congressional District by 35 to 20 percent with 40 percent undecided. The Uthlaut campaign questioned the validity of the poll because the sample was based on the overall population of the district rather than on past primary turnout (Rothenberg 1986b, 5). In North Dakota a 1986 poll conducted by Decision/Making/Information, Inc. (DMI) for the National Republican Senatorial Campaign Committee showed incumbent Republican senator Mark Andrews far ahead of his Democratic challenger. The Democrats charged that the sample under-represented Democrats, a criticism rejected by DMI (Rothenberg 1986b, 11). Andrews's reelection bid was unsuccessful.

Whatever the merits of the preceding criticisms, it is clear that the candidate "harmed" by the polls has strong incentives to undermine their credibility. If a campaign is not taken seriously, it will have difficulty in raising money and attracting other resources such as free media coverage. And one measure of the seriousness of a campaign is how it is faring in the polls. Hence, bad polling news must be vigorously counteracted by the campaign.

Sometimes candidates will deliberately manipulate aspects of their campaign or the polling process to generate results that will advance their candidacies. For example, in the four-man contest for the Republican nomination for governor of Ohio in 1982, one of the candidates, Seth Taft, timed his early television advertising to go on the air before the Ohio Republican party conducted a statewide poll assessing the standing of the candidates. The poll showed Taft running first, thereby enhancing his credibility. Undoubtedly, his famous last name and the skillful timing of his commercials gave Taft an early advantage in the polls, but he eventually lost the primary. To demonstrate greater electoral strength than they actually have, candidates often schedule television commercials and mailings in conjunction with party- and media-sponsored polls.

Candidates and campaign managers are also very skillful in selectively leaking information from in-house, private polls to improve their chances of winning. Sometimes these in-house polls are deliberately designed to generate desired results. For example, before asking the trial heat question about the contenders, they might ask a series of issue questions or candidate qualification items that will predispose the respondent to support one candidate over another. But in leaking the results of the trial heat item to the media, no information will be provided about the questions that preceded it. In addition, a candidate can try to manipulate the results by how the sample is selected. For example, if a candidate is thought to be more popular among women than men, the interviewing might be conducted mainly during the day to obtain a predominantly female sample. But when the results of the poll are leaked, no mention would be made of the gender composition of the sample, thereby inflating the standing of the candidate.

Voters and reporters should be wary of polling results selectively leaked by a campaign. One tipoff that something fishy may be going on

'You Blasted Idiot! I Keep Telling You I'm Feeling Fine!'

© Reprinted with permission.

is the refusal of the campaign to reveal additional information about the poll such as the question wording and question order. Although this kind of manipulation is not widespread, it does occur. The objective of most campaigns is to win, and many will utilize whatever tactics are felt to be helpful. One hopes that reporters and journalists will not be too easily victimized by campaigns and that citizens will exercise good judgment in evaluating election poll results.

Polls in the presidential selection process

Polls pervade all stages of the presidential selection process. During the general election, the major news organizations and the campaigns themselves regularly conduct polls. When a major campaign event occurs, such as a televised debate between the presidential contenders, a slew of polls follows immediately to assess its effect on the campaign. During the primary season, media polls in key states are common as are national polls measuring the presidential preferences of Democrats and Republicans throughout the nation.

The role of the pollster in presidential campaigns has become much more prominent in the past two decades with individual pollsters such as Pat Caddell and Richard Wirthlin achieving celebrity status during the Carter and Reagan campaigns. Pollsters today are part of the core strategy group that decides themes and tactics, media advertising, public speaking schedules, and other key aspects of the campaign.

The primary season

The combined effects of polls and media coverage of them are particularly critical during the primary season for a number of reasons. First, often many candidates seek the party's presidential nomination as witnessed by the Democrats in 1984 with eight contenders and the Republicans in 1980 with six. Unable to cover all candidates equally, the media give more attention to the most serious and viable candidates. Viability is defined by a candidate's standing in the polls.

Second, the primaries are a sequence of elections in which media coverage of the outcome in one state can dramatically affect later polls and primaries. For example, in 1984 John Glenn's campaign conducted a poll in New Hampshire about one week before that state's primary. The actual interviewing was done around the time of the Iowa precinct caucuses in which Glenn did much worse than expected. The media

106

coverage stressed how badly the Glenn campaign was hurt by the Iowa results. Glenn's New Hampshire survey showed that interviews completed before the reporting of his poor finish in Iowa had him running much more strongly in New Hampshire than did interviews completed after the reporting of the Iowa results. In general, because Iowa and New Hampshire have been the states that begin the formal delegate selection process, these primaries have received an inordinate amount of media coverage. The "winners" in Iowa and New Hampshire almost invariably enjoy a sizable gain in support in the national polls because of the positive and extensive media coverage they receive.

The presidential primary season can be viewed as a sequential, psychological game in which the perception that a candidate is running strongly as reflected in good poll results makes it easier to attract money, volunteers, and media coverage; bad poll results have the opposite effect. But strong performance in the polls is itself a function of the amount and content of the media coverage that a candidate receives. This is why Iowa and New Hampshire are so critical. Because they are small states in which both a personal and a media campaign can be conducted, they enable a relatively unknown candidate such as Jimmy Carter in 1976 or Gary Hart in 1984 to do better than expected and thus receive substantial media coverage. This coverage then results in the candidate moving up in the public opinion polls, which in turn further enhances the candidate's media coverage and credibility.

Polls become an overt part of campaign strategy during the primary season when candidates appeal for support on the grounds that they are more electable than their opponents as demonstrated by the polls. Probably the best examples of this phenomenon occurred in 1976 and 1968. In 1976 Gerald Ford and Ronald Reagan were locked in a tight battle for the Republican presidential nomination, the winner most likely having to face former Georgia governor Jimmy Carter in the fall. The Ford campaign conceded the South to Carter no matter who won the GOP nomination, but argued, citing public opinion polls, that Ford was the much stronger candidate to run against Carter nationwide (Phillips 1976).

Nelson Rockefeller's unsuccessful campaign to win the GOP nomination in 1968 heavily depended on the public opinion polls since he knew that he would have great difficulty winning presidential primaries and caucuses. Hence, Rockefeller challenged Richard Nixon, the frontrunner, to cosponsor fifty state polls to see which candidate was the strongest. Rockefeller also commissioned and released polls of key electoral vote states that showed him running better than Nixon against

Democratic candidate Hubert Humphrey (Crossley and Crossley 1969, 7). Rockefeller hoped to sway Republican delegates to his cause by the argument that he was the strongest candidate the party could offer.

Presidential debates

The interaction between poll results and media coverage is well illustrated by the treatment of the presidential and vice-presidential debates during the general election. Often polls taken immediately after a debate produce very different results than do polls taken a few days later, the difference being attributable to the dominant media message in the interim. For example, a CBS News/*New York Times* poll conducted immediately after the first Reagan-Mondale debate in 1984 showed that 43 percent thought Mondale won the debate, 34 percent thought Reagan won, and 16 percent saw it as a tie—a 9 percent Mondale advantage overall. But a CBS News/*New York Times* poll two days later gave Mondale a 49 percent advantage (66 percent thought the winner was Mondale, 17 percent Reagan, and 10 percent saw it as even). The only explanation for this massive shift in sentiment was the intervening news coverage of the debate that focused heavily on the president's poor performance and for the first time explicitly raised the question of the president's age. Citizens' responses in the second poll were highly influenced by what the media had to say about the debate.

Another example of influential media coverage is provided by polls conducted after the second Ford-Carter debate in 1976. In that debate President Ford made a blatant misstatement to the effect that Eastern Europe was not under the domination of the Soviet Union. Telephone polls immediately after the debate showed Carter winning, but only by a very narrow margin. Ford received negative media coverage after the debate for his mistake, and his campaign was not very skillful in putting the issue to rest when questioned by reporters as to what the president actually meant. As a result, polls taken a few days later showed that Americans overwhelmingly viewed Carter as the winner of the debate.

Hence, "winning" a debate may be less a matter of the candidate's actual performance and more a function of the media's coverage and interpretation of that performance. This is why the call-in poll sponsored by ABC News after the Carter-Reagan debate in 1980 was particularly offensive. ABC News invited its viewers to call one of two numbers to indicate whether they thought Reagan or Carter had won; the call cost fifty cents. Despite the self-selection and economic biases inherent in this procedure and the technical difficulty many citizens experienced in trying to complete their calls, ABC News announced that Reagan won the debate by a two-to-one margin over Carter. Ideally, Americans would have dismissed this instant poll as foolish and unsound. Unfortunately, because it was the first publicized, large-scale reaction to the debate, the poll and ABC's reporting of it shaped subsequent perceptions of who won the debate.

A final example of the role of polls in presidential debates occurred in 1980 when the League of Women Voters, the sponsor of the debate, decided to invite those candidates to participate in the debate whose popular support in public opinion surveys was more than 15 percent. The real issue was whether independent candidate John Anderson would be invited to participate. The Carter strategists wanted Anderson excluded since they believed that Anderson drew more votes from Carter than from Reagan, an effect that might be heightened if Anderson had the opportunity to share the same platform with Reagan and Carter. Anderson met the 15 percent test and had the chance to debate Reagan; Carter boycotted the debate. The League's use of polls in this fashion sparked much controversy among pollsters. The League was fortunate that Anderson clearly met the standard. What would the League have done had Anderson gotten only 13 percent? Would it have factored in sampling error? How would the League have treated the undecided respondents (Dionne 1980, E3; Knap 1980, 7)?

Conclusion

Polls do much more than simply reflect the current standing of the candidates in the presidential contest. The polls themselves and the reporting of them shape the very course of the campaign. But in one area the impact of the polls has been lessened—fund raising in the general election. Since 1976, presidential campaigns in the general election have been publicly funded. Major party nominees no longer need to worry that poor poll performance will cut off the flow of money to their campaigns. In 1968, however, many Democrats complained that early polls showing Humphrey losing badly hindered fund raising so that even when it became clear near the end of the campaign that Humphrey had a chance to win, the money available for the final push was inadequate. During the primary season, eligible candidates today receive only partial public funding. Public matching funds are contingent on the ability of the candidates to attract private financial support. Thus, bad poll results, as well as poor primary and caucus showings, may deter potential donors from supporting a failing campaign.

When and why election polls go wrong _____

It is somewhat unfair to emphasize the polls' errors in election prediction for in the vast majority of cases the polls are on target. Nevertheless, there have been notorious mistakes such as the *Literary Digest* poll of 1936 (discussed in Chapter 4) and the 1948 presidential election polls that indicated that Thomas E. Dewey would beat Harry S Truman. The bad call in 1948 is widely attributed to the quota method of sampling employed by the polls and more importantly to the fact that polling had stopped too far in advance of the election and therefore did not reflect the movement back to Truman of many would-be Democratic defectors. In fact, the last polls showed Dewey with only a five-point lead over Truman, and the trend in the polls had been one of a declining Dewey advantage.

The national polls in 1980 were widely criticized for not predicting the magnitude of Reagan's victory. Most polls showed a very tight race even though Reagan beat Carter by ten percentage points. Again the poor predictions were attributed to the fact that many polls did not continue right through to the end of the campaign and thus did not capture the last-minute surge to Reagan by the undecideds and independents. The state-level polls in 1980 were far more accurate in predicting a sizable Reagan victory. In 1982 the polls were widely criticized for projecting landslide victories for incumbent Republican governors in Illinois and Pennsylvania—the incumbent governors barely eked out a win—and for incorrectly predicting Tom Bradley would win in the California gubernatorial contest and Bill Clements's victory in the race for governor of Texas. Last-minute vote changes, emerging economic problems, and the inability to predict turnout accurately among various subgroups were all cited as explanations for the polls' faulty projections. This section examines four factors that affect election predictions: the timing of polls, the treatment of undecided voters, the estimation of
• turnout, and the changing political and economic climate.

The timing of polls

The timing of a preelection poll influences its accuracy; the closer to the election the poll is conducted, the more accurate its results are likely to be (Felson and Sudman 1975). The reasons for this are obvious. By definition, late polls can capture the effects of last-minute events and campaign activities that can markedly affect the outcome. In contrast, early polls primarily reflect name recognition and perceptions of incumbent performance. When voters have little information about the candidates, their attitudes about those candidates are highly volatile, assuming they acquire some new information about the contenders. This is why the presidential primary polls often have a poorer track record than do the general election polls. In the primaries, especially the early ones with a large field of candidates, information levels are low, and voters' commitment to candidates is weak.

The treatment of undecided voters

When respondents claim to be undecided they can mean different things. Some genuinely cannot choose among the candidates because they have sufficient, balanced information about them all that makes it difficult to opt for one; this is probably not a very common occurrence. Others may know very little about one or more of the candidates and therefore be unwilling or unable to make a choice. Finally, undecided may be a safe reply used by persons who do not want to reveal their already-made election choices to the interviewer.

Evidence for this third possibility is provided by the secret ballot technique long used by the Gallup Organization. In this procedure the respondent is given a ballot by the interviewer, asked to mark his or her choices, and then requested to drop the folded ballot into a box. Perry (1979) points out that this approach yields an undecided rate about one-third to one-fourth as large as would be obtained if respondents simply were asked their vote preference by means of a standard survey item. Note that the secret ballot technique can be used only with personal interviews. Hence, telephone interviews will often ask undecided respondents whether they lean to one candidate or another.

One way that pollsters may treat undecided respondents is simply to ignore them; results will be tabulated only for those respondents who have already made up their minds—a highly flawed procedure. Another way of handling the undecideds is to report their numbers, but then assume that the undecideds will split in the same way that the decideds already have. Thus, if the decideds vote 60 to 40 percent Democratic, the undecideds will be allocated 60 to 40 percent Democratic. This is probably a reasonable decision rule when both candidates are equally well known, and when there is no reason to suspect anything unique going on among the undecideds.

But when one candidate is well known and the other is not, then the treatment of the undecideds is more problematical. In a race between a well-known, long-term incumbent and a relatively unknown challenger, an undecided vote may reflect poorly on the incumbent. In 1978 I worked on the campaign of Ohio state representative Charles Kurfess who was challenging incumbent governor James Rhodes for the GOP gubernatorial nomination. Rhodes had already served three four-year terms as governor and was seeking his fourth. He was certainly the well-known warhorse of the Ohio Republican party. The benchmark survey done for the Kurfess campaign showed Rhodes favored over Kurfess by a 66-to-6 margin with 28 percent undecided. The final election results were 67 to 33 percent in favor of Rhodes. Without panel data one cannot definitively conclude that most of the undecideds moved to support Kurfess. Nevertheless, it seems plausible that the undecided vote in this case was actually a negative comment on the incumbent; in response to another question, the undecideds overwhelmingly preferred a new candidate for governor.

The 1986 contest for the Ohio GOP gubernatorial nomination illustrates the danger in ignoring undecideds. The candidates were James Rhodes, then seeking his fifth term as governor of Ohio, and state senators Paul Gillmor and Paul Pfeifer, who were not yet household names in the state. Most observers gave the two "Pauls" little chance to win since they were viewed as splitting the anti-Rhodes vote. At an important stage of the campaign, a major media-sponsored poll was released that received extensive coverage and showed Rhodes with 70 percent of the vote, Gillmor with 19 percent, and Pfeifer with 11 percent. The media coverage focused only on those respondents who had already made up their minds; moreover, the actual wording of the question did not include an undecided category: "Will you support James Rhodes, Paul Pfeifer, or Paul Gillmor for Governor in the Republican primary?" Nowhere in the newspaper reports of the poll (Miller 1986; Kostrzewa 1986b) was there any mention of the proportion of respondents who volunteered that they were undecided.

Ignoring the undecideds yielded a very high and widely publicized estimate of Rhodes's strength. The poll and the reporting of it unwittingly aided the Rhodes campaign by making his lead seem even more insurmountable and his nomination inevitable. Had undecideds been considered, Rhodes's nomination would not have been as much of a certainty, particularly if one believed that an undecided response in a choice between a sixteen-year former governor and two lesser known challengers was a negative reaction to that long-term incumbent. Ultimately, Rhodes, Gillmor, and Pfeifer received 48, 39, and 13 percent of the vote, respectively. The closeness of the outcome surprised many reporters and commentators and led them to wonder what might have happened had the Gillmor campaign been taken more seriously. But because of poll results like those described earlier, it was difficult for reporters to view the Gillmor effort as viable; hence, the dominant media focus was the inevitability of Rhodes's nomination. Rhodes lost badly in the general election.

Estimating turnout in elections

Probably the most difficult task pollsters face is estimating which of their respondents will actually vote. If the survey preferences of voters and nonvoters were identical, then this would not be a problem. But often there are marked differences between the two groups. Pollsters use a variety of means to predict whether a person will vote. The Gallup Organization has used a subsample of likely voters from the overall sample (Perry 1979, 320-321). Among the items used are the respondents' stated intention to vote, registration status, reported frequency of past voting, awareness of where to vote, interest in politics in general, interest in the particular election, and intensity of vote preference. Thus, in Gallup's final presidential election survey in 1976, when the entire set of respondents was included, Carter led Ford by 48 to 43 percent, with Eugene McCarthy and others receiving 4 percent, and undecideds and those who refused to participate 5 percent. But when likely voters only were considered, Carter led by only 48 to 46 percent, with 2 percent for other candidates and 4 percent undecided or refusing to respond to the poll.

Other pollsters use similar procedures for determining likely voters. For example, Peter Hart has used respondents' reports of registration status, past voting in other races and current intention to vote, interest in and perceived importance of the election, and awareness of the candidates and where to vote (Goldhaber 1984, 49). A somewhat different approach has been used by the *Columbus Dispatch*, which utilizes mailed questionnaires. As discussed in Chapter 4, mailed questionnaires have the problems of low response rates and uncertainty about the representativeness of those people who do reply. The *Dispatch* partially corrects for these problems by mailing questionnaires to samples selected from lists of registered voters who had voted in the past four primaries (Jordan 1982). This methodology is based on the social science notion that voting is a habitual activity and that the best predictor of current voting turnout is past voting participation. The *Dispatch* poll does not rely on respondents' own reports of their past voting behavior, which could suffer from faulty memory and deliberate

113

distortions as they try to portray themselves as conscientious citizens who voted even when they did not. Instead it uses highly accurate, official public records of past voter participation in elections. Of course, such records are not very helpful in estimating the likely turnout of newly registered voters.

The changing political and economic climate

Pollster Lance Tarrance observes that surveys will predict best when there is a normal voter turnout pattern. One reason why the polls performed so poorly in 1982 was that they consistently underestimated the Democratic turnout, which was higher that year than expected because of the deepening economic recession and the effective efforts by labor unions and black organizations to mobilize participation among their rank-and-file members. Moreover, although voter turnout is usually low among the unemployed, the 1982 election may have been atypical because many of the newly unemployed had been regular voters who therefore participated at a higher than expected rate in 1982 (Rothenberg 1983, 8).

Probably the contest that did the most damage to the polls' reputation in 1982 was the Illinois gubernatorial election. Most polls predicted that incumbent Republican governor James Thompson would score a smashing fifteen- to twenty-point victory over Adlai Stevenson (Day and Becker 1984; Kohut 1983). But when the votes were tabulated, Thompson narrowly won by less than 0.2 percent.

Day and Becker and Kohut tested numerous hypotheses concerning why the polls were so inaccurate. They ruled out some, such as last-minute shifts in preference that were missed by the polls; polls were conducted right to the very end of the campaign, and they still showed Thompson winning big. A poor estimate of the likely voters was also ruled out as the cause of the polls' inaccuracies. Instead, the polls' poor performance seemed to be caused mainly by an upsurge in straight-ticket voting among Democrats, including some Democrats who preferred Thompson to Stevenson but still cast a straight Democratic vote. In Chicago the Democratic organization devoted many resources to a "Punch 10" (that is, vote straight Democratic) media campaign, an effort that was particularly effective in black areas where it was part of an overall anti-Reagan theme (Day and Becker 1984, 613; Kohut 1983, 42). Thus, a good part of the Illinois poll debacle was due to political organization and mobilization, developments that are difficult to anticipate and assess by means of a poll.

Conclusion

There are many other ways in which election polls can go wrong, including poor question wording, bad samples, and incompetent interviewing. One hopes, of course, that these problems are not prevalent in a survey; if they were, one would have little confidence in the entire enterprise, let alone the specific election predictions. Even if the sample is a good one, citizens should be aware of the sample size and sampling error. One reason for the relatively poor performance of presidential primary polls is that they often have small samples and large sampling error (Mitofsky and Plissner 1980). Of fifty-one preprimary polls they analyzed, only five had a sampling error of three points or less; most had sample sizes of fewer than 500 with some having samples of 200 or fewer. A good preelection survey must successfully address all of the issues discussed in Chapters 2 through 5—nonattitudes, question wording, and sampling and interviewing techniques—as well as the unique problems inherent in making election predictions.

How preelection polls affect voters

Speculation about how polls affect voters has been widespread and contradictory. Some argue that polls that show one candidate ahead increase the incentives for supporters of the trailing candidate to change their preference and climb on board the winning candidate's bandwagon. Others emphasize not bandwagon effects but underdog effects; sympathetic voters, they claim, rally around the candidate whom the polls show to be losing. Little strong evidence supports either of these views. The bandwagon effect would require that leading candidates consistently increase their margin, while the underdog effect predicts that the losing candidate will inexorably gain on the leader. These simple kinds of effects have not shown up consistently in surveys.

An experimental study by de Bock (1976) found some evidence that the reporting of disheartening poll results weakened the support and turnout motivation among a candidate's adherents. However, this finding seems to be more a function of the experimental design itself in which exposure to the negative polls was much more direct than would be the case in the real-world setting. Other experimental studies have shown that polls can encourage support for the underdog, although the effects are not strong (Marsh 1984).

An ABC News/*Washington Post* poll in 1985 attempted to address the

115

PUBLIC OPINION POLLS DEFINITELY DO **NOT** INFLUENCE VOTERS!

I ADMIT OPINION POLLS **DO** INFLUENCE CAMPAIGN CONTRIBUTORS....

...AND CAMPAIGN SPENDING **DOES** INFLUENCE VOTERS...

ANYONE CAN CHANGE HIS OPINION

By Renault for McClatchy Newspapers

© Dennis Renault, *The Sacramento Bee.*

question of the effects of polls on vote choice. A sample of Americans was asked whether they were aware of whom the polls favored in 1984 and whether the polls had influenced their voting behavior (Sussman 1985f, 37). Seventy-eight percent correctly knew that the polls had picked Reagan to win, 7 percent said Mondale, and 15 percent did not know or remember what the polls had said. Among the 78 percent who knew the polls predicted a Reagan victory, 3.8 percent said it helped them decide for Reagan, 3.7 percent said it helped them decide for Mondale, and 92.5 percent said it had no effect. Sussman concluded that the preelection polls could not have had any significant impact on the vote split since the pro-Mondale and pro-Reagan effects almost cancelled each other.

Keep in mind three facts about Sussman's study. First, asking people to recall their views seven months after the election may generate many errors of memory. Second, Sussman's procedure requires people to remember explicitly that the polls had influenced them; polls could be influential without voters being consciously aware of it. Third, some people might not be willing to admit that the polls affected their vote choice lest they appear to be making decisions on inappropriate grounds. Despite these caveats, Sussman's conclusion seems plausible in general and certainly so for the 1984 election.

Bandwagon and underdog effects can and do occur, but their magnitude is small and probably inconsequential. Of course, polls may have an indirect effect on voters through their impact on campaign contributors, campaign workers, and media coverage, as illustrated by the Renault cartoon (above). In addition to voting behavior, polls can influence public opinion itself, a topic addressed in the last chapter. For example, if people become aware of changes in public opinion on an issue, that information may lead them to support the position favored by the trend. Or if they learn that their views are not shared by their fellow citizens, they may become unwilling to express their views. The very act of polling people may sensitize them to politics and campaigns and encourage them to seek out information and become more involved. Given the prominence of polls in elections and in political discourse in general, it is important for the citizen to be sensitive to the manipulative uses made of polls regardless of whether the manipulation is deliberate or unintentional.

Analyzing and interpreting polls ━━━━ 8

Thus far we have considered how public opinion surveys are conducted, how they are reported in the media, and how they influence elections and campaigns. This chapter focuses on the analysis and interpretation of poll data, the end products of a public opinion survey.

The interpretation of a poll is more an art than a science even though statistical analysis of poll data is central to the enterprise. In examining poll results the investigator has tremendous leeway in deciding which items to analyze, which sample subsets or breakdowns to present, and how to interpret the statistical results. For example, there may be three items in a poll that measure attitudes toward arms control negotiations. The analyst may construct an index from these three items as discussed in Chapter 3. Or the analyst may emphasize only the results from one question, perhaps because of space and time constraints and the desire to keep matters simple or because those particular results best support the analyst's own policy preferences. Likewise, the investigator may examine results from the entire sample and ignore subgroups whose responses may deviate from the overall pattern. Again time and space limitations or the investigator's own subjective preferences may influence these choices. Finally, two investigators can interpret identical poll results in sharply different ways depending upon what perspectives and values they bring to their data analysis; the glass may indeed be half full or half empty.

As the preceding examples suggest, analyzing and interpreting data is not an automatic, objective process, but instead one that entails a high degree of subjectivity and judgment. Subjectivity in most situations does not mean deliberate bias or distortion, but simply professional judgments about the importance and relevance of information. Certainly, news organizations' interpretations of their polls are generally done in

FRANK AND ERNEST 12-26-83-© Newspaper Enterprise Association, Inc.

an objective and unbiased fashion. But biases can slip in, sometimes unintentionally and sometimes deliberately as may occur when an organization has sponsored a poll in order to promote a particular position. This chapter presents a number of "mini" case studies that will illustrate the judgmental aspects of analyzing and interpreting poll results.

Choosing items to analyze

Many public opinion surveys are on multifaceted, complex issues. For example, one can query Americans about their attitudes toward tax reform and find that they overwhelmingly favor a fairer tax system. But if respondents are asked about specific aspects of tax reform, their answers may reflect high levels of confusion, indifference, or opposition. And depending upon which items are chosen for emphasis and reported, a picture of support, indifference, or opposition toward tax reform can be generated. American foreign policy in Central America is another highly complex subject that can elicit divergent reactions by Americans depending on which aspects of the policy they are questioned about.

Some surveys go into great depth on a topic with multiple items constructed to measure the various facets of the topic under investigation. The problem then becomes one of deciding which results to report. Often an extensive analysis will be conducted, but the media might publicize only a very abbreviated version. In such a case the consumer of the poll results is at the mercy of the media to portray accurately the overall study. Groups or organizations that sponsor polls to demonstrate support for a particular position or policy option often disseminate results in a selective fashion. This enables them to put the organization and its policies in a favorable light.

Other polls are more superficial in their treatment of particular topics because of their need to cover many subjects in the same survey. Such polls are labeled *omnibus surveys.* Here the problem becomes one of ensuring that the few questions employed to study a specific topic really do justice to the substance and complexity of that topic. The consumer of the poll is faced with the task of judging whether the survey has collected the most central information on the topic or whether other items might legitimately yield different substantive results.

A good example of how public opinion polling on a topic can be incomplete and potentially misleading is provided by the issue of prayer in public schools. Typically, pollsters ask Americans whether they support a constitutional amendment that would permit voluntary prayer in public schools, and more than three-fourths of Americans respond that they would favor such an amendment. I would argue that this question misses the mark. Voluntary prayer by individuals is in no way prohibited; the real issue is whether there will be *organized* voluntary prayer. But many pollsters do not include items that tap the organized aspects of voluntary prayer. Will there be a common prayer? If so, who will compose it? Will someone lead the class in prayer? If so, who? Under what circumstances and when will the prayer be uttered? What about students who do not wish to participate or prefer a different prayer?

The difficulty with either the in-depth or the omnibus survey is that the full set of items used to study a particular topic is usually not reported and hence the poll consumer cannot make informed judgments about whether the conclusions of the survey are valid. Therefore, claims by a corporate executive or an elected officeholder or a friend that the polls demonstrate public support or opposition to a particular position should be viewed skeptically. The obvious first question to ask is, What is the evidence cited to support the assertion? From there the citizen might examine the question wording, the response alternatives, the screening for nonattitudes, and the treatment of "don't know" responses. Then a more difficult task might be attempted, namely to assess whether the questions used to study the topic at hand were really optimal. What other questions might have been used? What aspects of the topic were not addressed? Finally, the citizen might ponder whether different interpretations could be imposed and whether alternative explanations could account for the observed patterns. In the remainder of this section we will discuss substantive examples that illustrate the importance of item selection.

There is always the temptation to seize upon those poll results that support one's position and ignore those that do not. The problem is that one or two items cannot capture the full complexity of most issues. For example, a *Newsweek* poll conducted by the Gallup Organization in July 1986 asked a number of questions about sex laws and lifestyles including the following three items (Alpern 1986, 38):

Do you approve or disapprove of the Supreme Court decision uphold-ing a state law against certain sexual practices engaged in privately by consenting adult homosexuals? [This question was asked of the 73 percent who knew about the Supreme Court decision.]

Disapprove	47%
Approve	41%

In general, do you think that states should have the right to prohibit particular sexual practices conducted in private between consenting adult homosexuals?

No	57%
Yes	34%

Do you think homosexuality has become an accepted alternative lifestyle or not?

Yes	32%
No	61%
Don't know	7%

Note that the first two items tap citizens' attitudes toward the legal treatment of homosexuals, while the third addresses citizens' views of homosexuality as a lifestyle. Although differently focused, all three questions deal with aspects of gay life. It would not be surprising to see gay rights advocates cite the results of the first two questions as indicating support for their position, while opponents of gay rights emphasize the third question.

An Eyewitness News/*Daily News* poll of New York City residents conducted in February 1986 further illustrates how the selective use and analysis of survey questions can generate very different impressions of popular opinion on an issue. In this poll a number of gay rights questions were asked:

On another matter, would you say that New York City needs a gay rights law or not?

Yes, need gay rights law	39%
No, do not need gay rights law	54%
Don't know/no opinion	8%

On another matter, do you think it should be against the law for landlords or private employers to deny housing or a job to someone because that person is homosexual or do you think landlords and employers should be allowed to do that if they want to?

Yes, should be against law	49%
No, should not be against law	47%

Volunteered responses

Should be law only for landlord	1%
Should be law only for employers	8%
Don't know/no opinion	3%

Although a definite majority of the respondents oppose a gay rights law in response to the first question, a plurality also believe that it should be illegal for landlords and employers to deny housing and jobs to persons because they are homosexual. Here the two questions both address the legal status of homosexuals, and it is clear which question gay rights activists and gay rights opponents would cite in support of their respective policy positions. It is not clear, however, which question is the better measure of public opinion. The first question is unsatisfactory because one does not know how respondents interpreted the scope of a gay rights law. Did they think it referred only to housing and job discrimination, or did they think it went substantially beyond that? The second question is inadequate if it is viewed as equivalent to a gay rights law. It also has the flaw of lumping housing and jobs together since citizens might have divergent views on these two aspects of gay rights.

Baron (1980, 21-24) compared the results of pairs of questions on various topics to show how question wording, none of it overtly loaded or biased, could generate highly dissimilar portraits of American public opinion. Following are pairs of items on four of the topics studied by Baron:

Détente

Harris Poll (June, 1978): Do you favor or oppose détente, that is the United States and Russia seeking out areas of agreement and cooperation?

Favor détente	69%
Oppose détente	19%

CBS News/*New York Times* Poll (June, 1978): What do you think the U.S. should do—should the U.S. try harder to relax tensions with the Russians or instead should it get tougher in its dealings with the Russians?

Relax tensions	30%
Get tougher	53%

123

SALT

Harris Poll (June, 1978): Do you favor or oppose the U.S. and Russia coming to a new SALT arms control agreement?

Favor SALT	72%
Oppose SALT	17%

Time/Yankelovich Poll (June, 1978): The government is attempting to negotiate a new agreement with Moscow called SALT II, limiting the number of strategic nuclear weapons either country will manufacture. Do you favor our signing this kind of agreement with the Russians or do you think it's too risky?

Favor SALT	32%
Oppose SALT	56%

Abortion rights

CBS News/*New York Times* Poll (October, 1977): The right of a woman to have an abortion should be left entirely to the woman and her doctor.

Agree	74%
Disagree	22%

Harris Poll (February, 1978): Do you support legalized abortion up to three months of pregnancy?

Yes	42%
No	40%

Pornography

CBS News/*New York Times* Poll (January, 1978): Should the government, at some level, restrict the sale of pornography to adults—or should adults be permitted to buy and read whatever they wish?

Restrict	44%
Don't restrict	56%

Time/Yankelovich Poll (November, 1977): The government should crack down more on pornography in movies, books and nightclubs.

Agree	74%
Disagree	23%

Note that most of these question pairs were asked at approximately the same time of year, so genuine attitude change probably does not account for the differences between the pairs of items. Instead, the differences can be attributed to question wording, response alternatives, and location of the question in the survey (although no information is provided about this in the Baron article).

Technically, there is no contradiction between the responses to the first pair of questions on détente; one can favor "seeking out areas of agreement and cooperation" with the Soviets on certain issues and getting "tougher with the Russians" on other issues. Nevertheless, it is easy to predict which result foreign policy liberals and conservatives would choose to support their respective policies for dealing with the Soviet Union.

The two items on SALT, the Strategic Arms Limitation Talks, are probably the most flawed, the first because many respondents will simply not know what a SALT arms control agreement entails and the second because of its highly leading response alternative of "or do you think it's too risky?" Again, two opposing policy stances could be supported, depending on the question cited. The third and fourth pairs on the lifestyle and civil liberties issues of abortion and pornography also demonstrate that ostensibly valid poll results can be found to support potentially conflicting issue positions.

An April 1986 CBS News/*New York Times* poll on U.S. policy toward Nicaragua further exemplifies how the choice of items can affect one's impression of American public opinion. Fifty-six percent of the sample thought "the government of Nicaragua threatens the security of other Central American countries," and 24 percent disagreed with this statement. Fifty-nine percent thought that "Nicaragua will provide military bases for the Soviet Union"; only 16 percent disagreed. Hence, a majority of Americans saw Nicaragua as a menace. And in response to the question "Do you think it is important to the security of the United States to eliminate Communism from Latin America, or can Communist governments exist in Latin America without threatening U.S. security?" 50 percent of the sample said it was important to eliminate Communism, 30 percent said that Communist governments did not necessarily threaten U.S. security, and 20 percent did not know. But when Americans were asked directly "Do you think the U.S. government should give $100 million in military and other aid to the Contras trying to overthrow the government in Nicaragua?" only 25 percent said yes, and fully 62 percent were opposed to the aid (and to the president's position).

Perhaps Americans believe that Nicaragua is a threat, but do not think that $100 million will solve the problem. Or citizens may be confused and ignorant on the issue. A series of CBS News/*New York Times* polls showed that even by April 1986, when the president had been talking for months about the threat posed by the Sandinista government of Nicaragua, only 38 percent of Americans knew that the

United States was supporting the side fighting against the Nicaraguan government. This 38 percent was double the level of awareness that existed just two years earlier. Moreover, the public's lack of knowledge as of April 1986 was further evidenced by responses to the question "Does Nicaragua have a Communist government, or a right-wing dictatorship, or does it have some other type of government?" Twenty percent replied Communist, 19 percent right-wing, 12 percent some other kind of government, and 49 percent did not know.

Examining trends with polling data

Polling data are often used to describe and analyze trends. This, of course, requires that the item(s) being investigated be included in multiple surveys conducted at different points in time. Ideally, the items would be identically worded. Yet even when questions are worded identically over time, serious problems of comparability may make trend analysis difficult. The identically worded item may not mean the same thing or provide the same stimulus to respondents because social and political changes in society have altered the meaning of the questions over time. For example, consider this question:

> Some say that the civil rights people have been trying to push too fast. Others feel they haven't pushed fast enough. How about you? Do you think that civil rights leaders are trying to push too fast, are going too slowly, or are they moving at about the right speed?

The responses to this item can be greatly influenced by the goals and agenda of the civil rights leadership at the time of the survey. A finding that more Americans think that the civil rights leaders are moving too fast or too slowly may reflect not a change in attitude from past views about civil rights activism but a change in the civil rights agenda itself. Follow-up questions designed to measure specific components of the civil rights agenda are needed.

There are other difficulties in achieving comparability over time. For example, even though the wording of an item remains the same, its placement within the questionnaire may change, which can alter the meaning of the question (see Chapter 3). Likewise, the definition of the sampling frame and the procedures used to achieve completed interviews may change. In short, comparability entails much more than simply having identically worded questions. Unfortunately, the consumer of polls is seldom provided sufficient information to judge whether items are truly comparable over time.

126

Examining subsets of respondents _____

Although it is natural to want to know the results from the entire sample, often the most interesting information in a poll comes from examining the response patterns of subsets of respondents defined according to certain theoretically or substantively relevant characteristics. For example, a January 1986 CBS News/*New York Times* poll showed President Ronald Reagan enjoying unprecedented popularity for a six-year incumbent: 65 percent approved of the president's performance, and only 24 percent disapproved. These overall figures mask some analytically interesting variations. For example, among blacks only 37 percent approved of the president's performance, and 49 percent disapproved. The sexes also differed in their views of the president, with men expressing a 72 percent approval rate compared with 58 percent for women. And as expected among categories of party loyalists, 89 percent of the Republicans, 66 percent of the independents, and only 47 percent of the Democrats approved of the president's performance. The discovery that blacks and whites or men and women differ in their views of the president prompts one to explore the reasons for these differences.

There is no necessary reason why public opinion on an issue should be uniform across subgroups. Indeed, on many issues there are reasons to expect just the opposite. Hence, in order to get a fuller understanding of American public opinion, it is important to examine the views of relevant subgroups of the sample. But as the sample is divided into subsets, the number of cases in each subset gets smaller, thereby increasing the sampling error and lowering the reliability of the sample estimates. For example, a sample of 1,600 Americans might be queried about their abortion attitudes. After the overall pattern is observed, one might wish to examine abortion attitudes within religious categories to determine whether religious affiliation is associated with attitudes toward abortion. Hence, the sample might be broken down by religion, yielding 1,150 Protestant, 400 Catholic, and 50 Jewish respondents. The analyst might observe that Catholics on the whole were the most opposed to abortion. To find out which Catholics are most likely to oppose abortion, the analyst might further divide the 400 Catholics into young and old Catholics, regular church attenders and nonregular attenders, or into the four categories of young Catholic churchgoers, old Catholic churchgoers, young Catholic nonattenders, and old Catholic nonattenders. The more breakdowns done at the same time, the quicker the sample size in any particular category plummets, perhaps leaving insufficient cases in some categories to make solid conclusions.

Innumerable examples can be cited to demonstrate the advantage of delving more deeply into poll data. An ABC News/*Washington Post* poll conducted in February 1986 showed major differences in the attitudes of men and women toward pornography; an examination of the total sample only would have missed these important divergences. In response to the question "Do you think laws against pornography in this country are too strict, not strict enough, or just about right?" 10 percent of the men said the laws were too strict, 41 percent said not strict enough, and 47 percent said about right. Among women, only 2 percent said the laws were too strict, a sizable 72 percent said they were not strict enough, and 23 percent thought they were about right (Sussman 1986c, 37).

A CBS News/*New York Times* poll of Americans conducted in April 1986 found widespread approval of the American bombing of Libya; 77 percent of the sample approved of the action, and only 14 percent disapproved. Despite the overwhelming approval overall, there were noteworthy differences among various subgroups. For example, 83 percent of the men approved of the bombing compared with 71 percent of the women. Of the white respondents, 80 percent approved in contrast to only 53 percent of the blacks (Clymer 1986c, A23). Even though all of these demographically defined groups gave at least majority support to the bombing, the differences in levels of support are both statistically and substantively significant.

School busing to achieve racial integration has consistently been opposed by substantial majorities in national public opinion polls. For example, a Harris poll commissioned by *Newsweek* in 1978 found that 85 percent of whites opposed busing (Williams 1979, 48). An ABC News/*Washington Post* poll conducted in February 1986 showed 60 percent of whites against busing (Sussman 1986b, 37). The difference between the two polls might reflect genuine attitude change about busing in that eight-year period, or it might be a function of different question wording or different placement within the questionnaire. Whatever the reason, additional analysis of both these polls shows that whites are not monolithic in their opposition to busing. For example, the 1978 poll showed that 56 percent of white parents whose children had been bused viewed the experience as "very satisfactory." The 1986 poll revealed sharp differences in busing attitudes among younger and older whites. Among whites aged thirty and under, 47 percent supported busing and 50 percent opposed it, while among whites over age thirty, 32 percent supported busing and 65 percent opposed. Moreover, among younger whites whose families had experienced busing firsthand, 54 percent approved of busing and 46 percent opposed it. (Of course, staunch opponents of busing may have moved to escape busing, thereby guaranteeing that the remaining population would be relatively more supportive of busing.)

Another example of the usefulness of examining poll results within age categories is provided by an ABC News/*Washington Post* poll conducted in May 1985 on citizens' views of how the federal budget deficit might be cut. One item read, "Do you think the government should give people a smaller Social Security cost of living increase than they are now scheduled to get as a way of reducing the budget deficit, or not?" Among the overall sample, 19 percent favored granting a smaller cost-of-living increase and 78 percent opposed. To test the widespread view that young workers lack confidence in the Social Security system and doubt they will ever get out of the system what they paid in, Sussman (1985d) investigated how different age groups responded to the preceding question. Basically, he found that all age groups strongly opposed a reduction in cost-of-living increases. Unlike in the busing example, no difference among age groups was discernible—an important substantive finding, particularly in light of the expectation that there would be divergent views among the old and young. Too often people mistakenly dismiss null (no difference) results as uninteresting and unexciting; a finding of no difference can be just as substantively significant as a finding of a major difference.

In many instances the categories used for creating subgroups are self-evident. For example, if one is interested in gender or racial differences, the categories of male and female or white and black are straightforward. Other breakdowns require more thought. For example, what divisions might one use to examine the effects of age? Should it be young, middle-age, and old? If so, what actual ages correspond to these categories? Is middle age thirty-five to sixty-five, forty to sixty, or what? Or should more than three categories of age be employed? In samples selected to study the effects of religion, the typical breakdown is Protestant, Catholic, and Jewish. But might not this simple threefold division overlook some interesting variations, particularly among Protestants of different denominations, some of which are evangelical, some fundamentalist, and others are not? Moreover, since most blacks are Protestants, comparisons of Catholics and Protestants that do not also control for race may be misleading. The consumer of polls should be sensitive to how pollsters define their subgroups because these definitions can affect the obtained results.

There are other variables for which the establishment of categories

is much more subjective and judgmental. For example, religious categories can be defined relatively easily by denominational affiliation as
mentioned earlier, but classifying respondents as evangelicals or fundamentalists is more complicated. Those who belong to denominations
normally characterized as evangelical or fundamentalist could be so
categorized. Or one might identify the beliefs of an evangelical or
fundamentalist, construct some polling questions, and then classify
respondents according to their responses to these questions. Obviously,
this requires some common core of agreement concerning the definition
of an evangelical or fundamentalist. Wilcox (1986, 6) argues:

> Fundamentalist and evangelicals have a very similar set of religious
> beliefs, including the literal interpretation of the Bible, the need for a
> religious conversion known as being "born-again," and the need to
> convert sinners to the faith. The evangelicals, however, are less anti-
> intellectual and more involved in the secular world, while the funda-
> mentalists criticize the evangelicals for failing to keep themselves "pure
> from the world."

Ideology is another example of a concept commonly used in
analyzing public opinion. The normal categories of ideology are liberal,
moderate, and conservative, and the typical way of obtaining this
information is to ask respondents a question in the following form:
"Generally speaking, do you think of yourself as a liberal, moderate, or
conservative?" One can raise many objections to this procedure including whether people really assign common meanings to these terms.
Indeed, the levels of ideological sophistication and awareness have been
an ongoing topic of research in political science.

Journalist Kevin Phillips (1981, B3) has cited the work of two
political scientists—Stuart A. Lilie and Williams S. Maddox—who argue
that the traditional liberal-moderate-conservative continuum is inadequate for analytical purposes. Instead, they propose a fourfold classifica-
tion of liberal, conservative, populist, and libertarian based upon two
underlying dimensions: whether one supports or opposes government
intervention in the economy and whether one supports or opposes
expansion of individual behavioral liberties and sexual equality. Liberals
were defined as persons who supported government intervention in the
economy and expansion of personal liberties, conservatives as persons
who opposed both, libertarians as citizens who favored expanding
personal liberties but opposed government intervention in the economy, and populists as persons who favored governmental economic
intervention but opposed the expansion of personal liberties. According
to one poll, populists comprised 24 percent of the electorate, conserva-

tives 18 percent, liberals 16 percent, and libertarians 13 percent with the rest of the electorate not readily classifiable or unfamiliar with ideological terminology.

This more elaborate breakdown of ideology may help us better understand public opinion, but the traditional categories still dominate political discourse. Thus, when one encounters citizens who oppose government programs that affect the marketplace but support pro-abortion court decisions, proposed gay rights statutes, and the Equal Rights Amendment, one feels uncomfortable calling them liberals or conservatives since they appear to be conservative on economic issues and liberal on lifestyle issues. But one might feel more confident in classifying them as libertarians.

Examining only the overall results of a survey can yield a technically accurate portrait of the public's views that is actually misleading; this can be illustrated by the public's reaction to the George Bush-Geraldine Ferraro vice-presidential debate in 1984. A CBS News/*New York Times* poll showed that 47 percent of the respondents thought Bush had won, 31 percent thought Ferraro had won, and 17 percent saw it as a tie. Many Reagan-Bush supporters trumpeted the poll results as evidence that their candidate had won and was therefore the better choice. Fortunately, the numbers reported by the media went beyond the simple overall result and provided the following information (Raines 1984, 1e):

Who won the debate?	Candidate preference		
	Reagan-Bush	Mondale-Ferraro	Undecided
Ferraro	4%	73%	19%
Bush	76	5	22
Tie, don't know	20	22	59

Note that 76 percent of the Reagan-Bush supporters thought Bush had won, while 73 percent of the Mondale-Ferraro supporters thought Ferraro had won. Hence, Bush and Ferraro were evaluated almost equally positively by their own partisans. And among the undecided respondents, the verdict on the debate was a virtual draw with 22 percent saying Bush had won, 19 percent Ferraro, and most of the rest calling it a tie. Obviously, then, the reason why Bush enjoyed a

131

substantial 47-to-31 advantage in the entire sample was simply because the sample had more respondents who before the debate were for Reagan-Bush rather than for Mondale-Ferraro. Social psychological theories suggest that debates tend to reinforce viewers' preexisting candidate preferences (Sigelman and Sigelman 1984). That certainly seems to have been the case for the Bush-Ferraro encounter. The media stories generally pointed this out, although one unfortunate aspect of the reporting of the CBS News/*New York Times* poll was that nowhere in the news release prepared by CBS News or in two *New York Times* articles on the poll was the reader ever presented the complete three-by-three table along with the number of cases on which the percentages were calculated.

A final example of the importance of examining subsets of respondents is provided by a January 1985 ABC News/*Washington Post* poll that queried Americans about their attitudes on a variety of issues and presented results, not only for the entire sample, but also for subsets of respondents defined by their attentiveness to public affairs (Sussman 1985b, 37). Attentiveness to public affairs was measured by whether the respondents were aware of four news events: the subway shooting in New York City of four alleged assailants, the switch in jobs by Donald Regan and James Baker, the Treasury Department's proposal to simplify the tax system, and anti-apartheid protests in the United States. Respondents then were divided into four levels of awareness with 27 percent in the highest category, 26 percent in the next highest, 25 percent in the next category, and 22 percent falling in the lowest. The next step in the analysis was to compare the policy preferences of the highest and lowest awareness subsets.

There were some marked differences between these two groups. For example, on the issue of support for the president's military buildup, 59 percent of the lowest awareness respondents said that there should not be any major cuts in military spending in order to lessen the budget deficit. In contrast, 57 percent of the highest awareness group said that military spending should be limited in order to help with the budget deficit. On the issue of tax rates, a majority of both groups agreed with the president that taxes were too high, but there was a sizable difference in each majority. Among the lowest awareness respondents, 72 percent said taxes were too high and 24 percent said they were not, while among the highest awareness respondents, 52 percent said taxes were too high and 45 percent said they were not (Sussman 1985b, 37).

These findings raise some interesting normative issues about public opinion polls. As mentioned in Chapter 1, the methodology of public opinion polls is very democratic. All citizens have a nearly equal chance to be selected in a sample and have their views counted; all respondents are weighted equally (or nearly so) in the typical data analysis. Yet except at the polls all citizens do not have equal influence in shaping public policy. The distribution of political resources, be they financial or informational, is not uniform across the population. Polls themselves become a means to influence public policy as various decision makers cite poll results to legitimate their policies. But should the views of all poll respondents be counted equally? An elitist position would argue that the most informed segments of the population should be given the greatest weight. Therefore, in the preceding defense spending example, more attention should be given to the views of the highest awareness subset (assuming the validity of the way in which the levels of awareness were constructed), which was more supportive of reducing military spending. An egalitarian argument would assert that all respondents should be counted equally. We will return to the role of the polls in a democratic political system in the last chapter.

Interpreting poll results

An August 1986 Gallup poll on education showed that by a 67 to 24 percent margin Americans would allow their children to attend class with a child suffering from acquired immune deficiency syndrome (AIDS). What reaction might there be to this finding? Some might be shocked and depressed that almost one-fourth of Americans could be so mean spirited toward AIDS victims when the scientific evidence shows that AIDS is not a disease transmitted by casual contact. Others might be reassured and relieved that two-thirds of Americans are sufficiently enlightened or tolerant to allow their children to go to school with AIDS victims. Yet a third response might be dismay; how could 67 percent of Americans foolishly allow their children to go to school with an AIDS victim when there is no absolute guarantee that AIDS cannot be transmitted casually?

Or consider this example of how the same data can be interpreted differently. The following item was used in a 1983 poll by the National Opinion Research Center (NORC): "If your party nominated a black for President, would you vote for him if he were qualified for the job?" Eighty-five percent of the white respondents said yes. How might this be interpreted? One way would be to feel positive about how much racial attitudes have changed in the United States. A different perspec-

tive would decry the fact that in this supposedly tolerant and enlightened era, 15 percent of white survey respondents could not bring
themselves to say they would vote for a qualified black candidate.

In both the AIDS and black presidential candidate examples, there
is no single correct meaning to be assigned to the data. Instead, the
interpretation chosen will be a function of the values and beliefs of the
poll consumer and the purposes that he or she has in analyzing the
survey. For the rest of this section, we will address the interpretation of
public opinion polls by citing specific substantive examples.

The first example comes from an analysis of two national surveys on
gun control, one sponsored by the National Rifle Association and
conducted by Decision/Making/Information, Inc. (DMI) and the other
sponsored by the Center for the Study and Prevention of Handgun
Violence and done by Cambridge Reports, Inc. (Patrick Caddell's firm).
Not surprisingly, the two reports arrived at substantively different
conclusions. The NRA's analysis concluded:

> Majorities of American voters believe that we do *not* need more laws
> governing the possession and use of firearms and that more firearms
> laws would *not* result in a decrease in the crime rate. (Wright 1981, 25)

In contrast, the Center's report stated:

> It is clear that the vast majority of the public (both those who live with
> handguns and those who do not) want handgun licensing and registra-
> tion.... [T]he American public wants some form of handgun control
> legislation. (Wright 1981, 25)

Wright carefully analyzed the evidence cited in support of each conclusion and found that

> the major difference between the two reports is not in the findings, but
> in what is said about or concluded about the findings: what aspects of
> the evidence are emphasized or de-emphasized, what interpretation is
> given to a finding, and what implications are drawn from the findings
> about the need, or lack thereof, for stricter weapons controls. (Wright
> 1981, 38)

In essence, the statistical results from both surveys were very comparable; it was what was done with the data that generated the difference in
the substantive recommendations.

Two polls on tax reform provide another example of how poll data
can be selectively interpreted and reported (Sussman 1985a, 37). The
first poll was sponsored by the insurance industry and was conducted by
pollster Burns Roper. Its main conclusion, reported in a press conference
announcing the poll results, was that 77 percent of the American public
"said that workers should not be taxed on employe benefits" and only

15 percent supported such a tax, a conclusion very reassuring to the insurance industry.

However, Roper included other items in the poll that the insurance industry chose not to emphasize. As Sussman points out, the 77 percent opposed to the taxing of fringe benefits were then asked, "Would you still oppose counting the value of employe benefits as taxable income for employes if the additional tax revenues went directly to the reduction of federal budget deficits and not into new spending?" Twenty-six percent were no longer opposed to taxing fringe benefits, bringing the overall opposition down to 51 percent of the sample. A second follow-up question was asked, "Would you still oppose counting the value of employe benefits as taxable income for employes if the additional tax revenues permitted an overall reduction of tax rates for individuals?" a feature that was part of the Treasury Department's initial tax proposals. Now only 33 percent of the sample was opposed to taxing fringes, 50 percent supported it, and 17 percent were undecided. Thus, depending upon which results one used, one could show a majority of citizens supportive or opposed to taxing fringe benefits.

The second poll that Sussman analyzed also tapped people's reactions to the Treasury Department's tax proposal. A number of questions in the survey demonstrated public hostility to the Treasury proposal. One item read:

> The Treasury Department has proposed changing the tax system. Three tax brackets would be created, but most current deductions from income would be eliminated. Non-federal income taxes and property taxes would not be deductible, and many deductions would be limited. Do you favor or oppose this proposal? (Sussman 1985a, 37)

Not surprisingly, 57 percent opposed the Treasury plan, and only 27 percent supported it. But as Sussman points out, the question is highly selective and leading since it focuses on changes in the tax system that hurt the taxpayer. For example, nowhere does it inform the respondent that a key part of the Treasury plan was to reduce existing tax rates so that 80 percent of Americans would be paying either the same amount or less in taxes than they were paying before. Clearly, this survey was designed to obtain a set of results compatible with the sponsor's policy objectives.

Our final example of the consequences of poll interpretation comes from a recent controversy generated by Linda Lichter's article "Who Speaks for Black America?" Samples of 600 black Americans and 105 black leaders were interviewed. The surveys revealed "a surprising divergence between black leaders and the average black American on a broad spectrum of concerns, including some at the very heart of race relations" (Lichter 1985, 41). Williams (1985, A-11) and Sussman (1985g, 37) critized Lichter's methodology, but I would argue that the major flaw of her research is that its implicit conclusions are not supported by the evidence and arguments.

Lichter's article begins with the observation that civil rights leaders and the Reagan administration have been accusing each other of racism. She then cites the views of Clarence Pendleton, the black chairman of the U.S. Civil Rights Commission and a supporter of President Reagan, who "has labeled traditional civil rights advocates as 'media-designated black leaders' who advocate a 'new racism' by promoting preferential treatment for minorities." She also cites the views of traditional black leaders who see the Reagan administration as being insensitive to the situation of black Americans. She labels these two sets of contending opinions a debate and states that underlying it are "some critical assumptions about race relations in this country." She then states that her study, which investigates the views of black leaders and citizens, will fill in gaps in our knowledge about blacks' attitudes on "problems that have set the leaders against one another" (Lichter 1985, 41).

Thus, for Lichter, there are seemingly two sets of leaders, the traditional black leaders and the Reagan administration (and its white and black spokesmen). Presumably, if traditional black leaders are not in agreement with black citizens that would undermine the traditional black leadership and enhance the standing of the Reagan administration in the ongoing debate. Although this argument is not explicitly made, it is a reasonable interpretation given the way that Lichter has framed her research question.

But Lichter does not directly speak to the issue. Even if traditional black leaders and black citizens do not agree on some issues, this does not discredit black leaders who are critical of the Reagan administration and its policies. There is an implicit litmus test in her research that black leaders must agree with followers in order to be viewed as legitimate representatives. If so, it would be necessary to compare also the attitudes of white citizens with the views of the white political leadership, especially representatives of the Reagan administration.

If her objective was to determine which group of leaders better represented black citizens, her research should have been designed to do that more directly. As it is, there are two items in her survey of black citizens that directly measure attitudes toward the president and traditional black leaders and two other items that tap opinions of the Democratic and Republican parties. Although the rank-and-file black sample is not as hostile to the president and the GOP as are the black leaders, nevertheless 70 percent of black citizens (compared with 87 percent of the leaders) disapproved of Reagan's performance as president. Moreover, 58 percent of blacks believed that the Republican party is "less interested in helping to solve the problems of black America as compared with four years go"; only 28 percent said the same about the Democratic party. (For black leaders, 59 and 74 percent see the Democratic and Republican parties respectively as having become less sympathetic to blacks.) Finally, in response to the question "Do you think that the black leaders you see on TV newscasts and read about in the newspapers are generally speaking for the majority of black people, or do you think they usually speak for only a minority of black people?" 52 percent of black citizens thought these black leaders spoke for a majority of blacks.

Lichter's research may have some methodological flaws. These include questions on which black citizens might feel pressured to give socially desirable responses about opposing preferential treatment, loaded questions that might have affected the responses of black citizens more than those of black leaders, and a lack of sophistication about why leaders might have responded strategically to some of the simplistic survey questions. But the real problem with her research is that it is used to address a question about which it has relatively little to say: Who speaks for black Americans? Had she simply wanted to compare the attitudes of black Americans and black leaders, her research would not have been nearly so controversial. It is the implicit conclusions that are drawn from her research about the broader issue of who represents the views of black Americans that get her into trouble. Unfortunately, this is a fairly common problem in public opinion research. The results of a survey designed for one particular purpose are often inappropriately applied to topics and questions that the survey was not designed to study.

Weighting the sample

As explained in Chapter 4, samples are selected to be representative of the broader population from which they are drawn. Sometimes adjustments must be made to a sample before the analysis is done and the results reported. These adjustments may be made for substantive reasons or because of biases in the characteristics of the selected sample. An example of the former is pollsters' attempts to determine who the likely voters will be and to base their election predictions, not on the entire sample, but on the subset of likely voters.

To correct for biases, weights can be used so that the sample's demographic characteristics more accurately reflect the population's overall properties. Because sampling and interviewing entail statistics and probability theory as well as logistical problems of contacting respondents, the sample may contain too few blacks, or too few men, or too few people in the youngest age category, for example. Assuming that one knows the true population proportions for gender, race, and age, one can adjust the sample by the use of weights to bring its numbers into line with the overall population values. For example, if females constitute 60 percent of the sample but 50 percent of the overall population, one might weight each female respondent by five-sixths, thereby reducing the percentage of females in the sample to 50 percent (five-sixths times 60 percent).

A 1986 *Columbus Dispatch* preelection poll on the gubernatorial preferences of Ohioans illustrates the consequences of weighting. In August 1986 the *Dispatch* sent a mail questionnaire to a sample of Ohioans selected from the statewide list of registered voters. The poll showed that incumbent Democratic governor Richard Celeste was leading former GOP governor James Rhodes by 48 to 43 percent with independent candidate and former Democratic mayor of Cleveland Dennis Kucinich receiving 9 percent; undecideds were not allowed (Curtin 1986a, 1A). Fortunately, the *Dispatch* report of its poll included the sample size for each category (unlike the practice of the national media). One table presented to the reader showed the following relationship between political party affiliation and gubernatorial vote preference (Curtin 1986b, 8E):

Gubernatorial preference	Party affiliation		
	Democrat	Republican	Independent
Celeste	82%	14%	33%
Rhodes	9	81	50
Kucinich	9	5	17
Total %	100	100	100
(N)	(253)	(245)	(138)

Given the thrust of the news story that Celeste was ahead by 48 to 43 percent, the preceding numbers were surprising since Rhodes was running almost as well among Republicans as Celeste was among Democrats, and Rhodes had a substantial lead among independents. Because the *N*s were provided, one could calculate the actual number of Celeste, Rhodes, and Kucinich votes in the sample as follows:

$$\text{Celeste votes} = .82(253) + .14(245) + .33(138) = 287$$
$$\text{Rhodes votes} = .09(253) + .81(245) + .50(138) = 291$$
$$\text{Kucinich votes} = .09(253) + .05(245) + .17(138) = 58$$

Calculating percentages from these totals shows Rhodes ahead by 46 to 45 percent rather than trailing by 48 to 43 percent. At first I thought there was a mistake in the poll or in the party affiliation and gubernatorial vote preference. In rereading the news story, however, I learned that the sample had been weighted. The reporter wrote, "Results were adjusted, or weighted, slightly to compensate for demographic differences between poll respondents and the Ohio electorate as a whole" (Curtin 1986b, 8). The reporter did inform the reader that the data were weighted, but nowhere did he say that the adjustment affected who was ahead in the poll.

The adjustment probably was statistically valid since the poll respondents did not seem to include sufficient numbers of women and blacks, two groups that were more supportive of the Democratic gubernatorial candidate. However, nowhere in the news story was any specific information provided on how the weighting was done. This example illustrates that weighting can be consequential, and it is probably typical in terms of the scant information provided to the citizen about the weighting procedures that were employed.

When polls conflict: a concluding example _____

A good way to conclude this chapter is to review a variety of factors that can influence poll results and their subsequent interpretation. A useful vehicle for this endeavor is the preelection polls in the 1980 and 1984 presidential elections, polls that were often highly inconsistent. For example, in the 1984 election various polls done at comparable times yielded highly dissimilar results. A Harris poll had Reagan leading Mondale by nine percentage points, an ABC News/*Washington Post* poll had Reagan ahead by twelve points, a CBS News/*New York Times* survey had Reagan leading by thirteen points, a *Los Angeles Times* poll gave Reagan a seventeen-point lead, and an NBC News poll had the president ahead by twenty-five points (Oreskes 1984, A8). A similar situation

Summary of . . .

Designing a "perfect" poll is a bit like creating the "perfect" spaghetti sauce: all cooks start with tomatoes, but each uses his own favorite combination of seasonings—sometimes with widely varied results. Presented below are the ingredients that went into the survey designs of four major national polling organizations this past election year. . . .

CBS/New York Times

Population sampled from: National adult population telephone survey.

Household selection: Random digit dialing. Up to four attempts to contact household.

Respondent selection: Random selection, appointment made if designated respondent not at home.

Weighting: To correct for household size and to reflect demographics.

Identification of electorate: "Likelihood weight" based on past voting behavior and current intention and reported behavior of similar groups in 1976.

Actual choice: Choice among three major candidates, labeled by party. Leaners included in reported distributions.

Adjustments: None.

Gallup

Population sampled from: Registered voters. In-person interviews.

Household selection: Households randomly selected from sample precincts. No callbacks.

Respondent selection: Systematic selection based on age and sex.

Weighting: To correct for "times at home" and to reflect demographics.

Identification of electorate: "Likely voters" identified based on past behavior, interest, and intention to vote, and expected turnout.

Actual choice: "Secret ballot" for tickets, labeled by party. Undecided asked to mark ballot based on leaning.

Adjustments: Undecideds allocated; figures corrected for deviation of sample precincts from national results in 1976.

ABC/Harris*

Population sampled from: Expected electorate (based on 1976). Series of telephone surveys.

Household selection: Random digit dialing. Households not reached retained for one more survey.

Respondent selection: Systematic selection by modified sex quota.

Weighting: To reflect demographics.

Identification of electorate: "Likely voters" identified based on past behavior and intention to vote, and expected turnout.

Actual choice: Choice among three major candidates, labeled by party. Leaners included in reported distributions.

Adjustments: Survey results from last 12 days combined. (No day-to-day differences noted). Undecided allocated evenly between Carter and Reagan.

... Polling Methodology

NBC/AP**

Population sampled from: National adult population. Telephone survey.
Household selection: Random digit dialing. No callbacks (except for "busies").
Respondent selection: Systematic selection based on sex quota.
Weighting: None. Sample deemed "self-weighting."
Identification of electorate: "Likely voters" identified based on past behavior, interest, and intention to vote.
Actual choice: Choice among three major candidates, labeled by party (following questions on open-ended preferences and whether respondents had made up minds).

Adjustments: None.

Glossary

National adult population. The sample is designed to reflect the characteristics, including geographic distribution, of the entire adult population.
Registered voters. The same, but the population is registered voters, instead of all adults.
Electorate. The same, but the actual electorate—i.e. taking differential turnout on a geographic basis into account.
Random digit dialing. Procedures giving households (both listed and unlisted numbers) a fair chance to be reached.
Callbacks. Multiple attempts to reach a household.
Random selection. Procedures to give each potential respondent in a household a random chance to come into the sample.
Systematic selection. Selection according to same system, depriving the interviewer of the choice of respondent.
Likelihood weight. An estimate of how likely someone is to vote. Someone who is 80 percent likely will count twice as much in the final figures as someone only 40 percent.
Likely voters. An attempt to separate respondents into two groups: "likely voters" and "non-likely voters." Only the former enter into the reported distributions.
Allocation. Division of the undecided based on other information, such as their partisan preference, issue positions, or data from other surveys.

Note: This overview cannot capture the full details of procedures used—for example what precise "demographics" were used.
* ABC had conducted polls with Louis Harris and Associates at the time of this summary. ** AP conducted a survey on its own after the last joint survey.

Source: C. Everett Ladd and G. Donald Ferree, "Were the Pollsters Really Wrong?" *Public Opinion,* vol. 3, no. 6 (December/January 1981): 18. Reprinted with permission of American Enterprise Institute.

occurred in 1980, although the disparity among the polls was not as great. How can polls on an ostensibly straightforward topic such as presidential vote preference differ so widely? Many reasons can be cited, some obvious and others more subtle in their effects.

Among the more subtle reasons are the method of interviewing and the number of callbacks that a pollster employs to contact respondents who initially were unavailable. According to Lewis and Schneider (1982, 43), pollsters Patrick Caddell and George Gallup found that Reagan received less support from respondents interviewed personally than from those queried over the telephone. The speculative explanation for this finding was that weak Democrats who were going to desert Carter found it easier to admit this in a telephone interview than in a face-to-face situation. With respect to callbacks, Dolnick (1984, C1) reports that one reason why the Harris poll was closer than others in predicting Reagan's sizable victory in 1980 was that it made repeated callbacks that at each stage "turned up increasing numbers of well-paid, well-educated Republican-leaning voters."

Some of the more obvious factors that help account for differences among the polls are question wording and question placement. Some survey items mention the presidential and vice-presidential candidates; others mention only the former. Some pollsters ask follow-up questions of undecided voters to ascertain whether they lean toward one candidate or another; others do not. Question placement can also be consequential. Normally, incumbents and better known candidates do better when the vote intention question is asked at the beginning of the survey rather than later. If vote intention is measured after a series of issue and problem questions have been asked, respondents may have been reminded of shortcomings in the incumbent's record and therefore be less willing to express support for the incumbent.

There are differences among polls in how the sample is selected and how it is treated for analytical purposes. Some polls sample registered voters; others query adult Americans. There are differences in the methods used to identify likely voters, as discussed in Chapter 7. As Lipset (1980) points out, the greater the number of respondents who are screened out of the sample because they do not seem to be likely voters, the more likely the remaining respondents will be relatively more Republican in their vote preferences. Some samples are weighted to guarantee demographic representativeness; others are not.

It is also possible that discrepancies among polls are not due to any of the above factors, but simply reflect statistical fluctuations. For example, if one poll with a 4 percent sampling error shows Reagan ahead of Mondale by 52 to 43 percent, this result is statistically congruent with other polls that might have a very narrow 48 to 47 percent Reagan lead or other polls that show a landslide 56 to 39 percent Reagan lead.

The box on pages 140-141 presents a summary of some of the major features of the 1980 election polls. As the summary makes clear, many factors affect the data reported by the media even if the reader or viewer is not given information about each of them. In addition to the influences listed in the box are the values and goals of the public opinion analyst. As we have shown in this chapter, the interpretation of poll data can be a highly subjective enterprise that is affected by the perspective and the intentions of the investigator. Hence, public opinion polling is a complex activity subject to many influences that can alter the substantive results. It thus behooves the consumer of opinion polls to examine them in a critical and questioning fashion. Informed skepticism is an appropriate posture to take with respect to the polls; uninformed hostility or unthinking acceptance is not.

Advice to poll consumers　9

It's very clear
The polls are here to stay;
Not for a year,
But ever and a day.

The interviews and the questionnaires
And the pollsters that we know
Aren't just passing fancies—
Oh, my goodness, no!

The media
Love polls in every way.
It matters not
If polls have scant to say.

In time statistics may numb you,
Results may stun you.
Wait for another day,
For—the polls are here to stay.

— with apologies to George Gershwin

To death and taxes should be added public opinion polls, an integral and unavoidable part of American society today. Public opinion polling is a contemporary manifestation of classical democratic theory; it emphasizes the ability of the rational and wise citizen to make informed judgments on the major issues of the day. Hence, political organizations that can demonstrate that public opinion is on their side enjoy an advantage as they promote their ends. News organizations have also become enamored of the polls, in part because polls seem to elevate the citizen (and thus the media audience) to a more prominent political role: in effect, the polls convert the amorphous citizenry into a unified actor in the political process. Poll results that are not supportive of government actions provide the media with stories of conflict between the government and the people, just as the media focus on points of contention between the president and the Congress or between the House and the Senate.

As the technology of polling has been continually refined, upgraded, and made more available, the ability to sponsor and conduct polls has spread to many institutions and organizations throughout American society. Today private groups and organizations can readily hire pollsters to conduct surveys that will promote their aims. If these organizations want to be absolutely sure that the poll results will be favorable, they can conduct their own surveys replete with loaded questions, skewed samples, and faulty interpretations.

The major news organizations have heavily invested in their own in-house polling operations with the result that the number of polls conducted have increased in order to justify this investment and to keep up with the competition. For certain news stories, such as presidential debates, the failure to conduct and report a poll on who won would leave a news organization open to the criticism of incomplete news coverage. The unseemly contest among the media to be the first to "call" the outcome of particular elections illustrates how the pressures of competition and ratings promote the widespread use of polls. The media operate under the assumption that the public reactions to major news events are meaningful and that public opinion polls enhance the news value of a story.

How to evaluate polls: a summary _____

Polls are a meaningful way for citizens to participate in society and to become informed about the relationship between the decisions of government and the opinions of its citizenry. As more organizations conduct polls and disseminate their results in order to inform and to sway public opinion, citizens should become pickier consumers, sensitive to those factors that can affect poll results. The acquisition of this sensitivity does not require familiarity with statistics or survey research experience. Consumers need only treat polls with a healthy skepticism and keep in mind the following questions as tools to evaluate poll results.

One basic question that poll consumers should ask is whether the public opinion survey is measuring genuine opinions or nonattitudes. Are respondents likely to be informed and have genuine opinions about the topic? Or is the focus so esoteric that their responses largely reflect the social pressures of the interview situation to provide answers even when they have no real views on the subject at hand? The answers to these questions are not easy for, as W. Russell Neuman argues, there is often not a clear demarcation between attitudes and nonattitudes. Indeed, Neuman coined the term *quasi-attitude*—something between an attitude and a nonattitude—and points out that citizens' responses to survey questions are "a mixture of carefully thought out, stable opinions, half-hearted opinions, misunderstandings, and purely random responses" (Neuman 1986, 184). Another question to consider is whether the researchers have made any effort to screen out respondents who lack genuine attitudes on the topic. Unfortunately, information about prior screening questions and their effects are frequently not reported. Often one cannot tell what proportion of the total sample has answered a particular item and what proportion has been screened out. News organizations should do a better job reporting this information. At the minimum, they should provide the number of respondents who answer a particular question. When this number is substantially smaller than the total sample size, they should explain this discrepancy.

Because screening information is often not presented, the citizen is forced to form impressionistic judgments about whether the measurement of nonattitudes has been a problem in the survey. Of course, some issues of public policy, even issues such as tax reform that have been hotly debated and contested by political elites, may not be of much interest to many Americans and thus may be highly susceptible to the measurement of nonattitudes.

Since the actual wording of questions is usually reported, citizens are in a better position to evaluate the potential effects of question wording than the presence of nonattitudes. Citizens can certainly judge whether there are any blatantly loaded words or phrases in the questions, whether the alternatives are presented in a fair and balanced fashion, and whether the overall question accurately reflects the topic under study. If the question wording is omitted, particularly on items dealing with controversial issues, the poll consumer should be wary and ask why.

Unfortunately, assessing the effects of the overall question order is more difficult since the complete questionnaire is seldom provided in press releases (other than those issued by news organizations) and in news stories. Moreover, the fact that earlier questions can affect responses to subsequent queries is a subtle phenomenon for which most citizens have little intuitive feel. Yet the strategic placement of questions is one of the most effective ways to "doctor" a survey. While each individual question may be balanced and fair, the overall order of the questions may stimulate specific responses preferred by the sponsor of the survey. One clue that this problem may exist is the refusal of an organization, such as a political campaign team, to release the entire poll results after it has released a few results that show it in a favorable light.

The most mysterious part of polling for most Americans—sampling—is probably the least important for them to understand in detail. Reputable pollsters pick good samples and typically report the sampling error and confidence level so that the poll consumer can form independent judgments about the significance of the results. To make sure that the sample properly reflects the aims of the poll, the poll consumer should pay close attention to how the sample is defined. And certainly the consumer should confirm that the sample is a scientifically selected probability sample rather than a purposive sample that the investigator selected for reasons of convenience.

One aspect of sampling that citizens should not overlook is the proportion of the total sample to which a particular finding applies. For a variety of reasons, such as the use of screening questions or the need to study analytically interesting subsets of the original sample, the proportion of respondents on which a result is based may be substantially smaller than the overall sample. Thus, one should know not only the sampling error of the total sample, but also the sampling error of the subsets.

It is almost impossible for the citizen to evaluate the effects of interviewing on poll results since too little information is usually provided about the interviewing process beyond the method of interviewing (for example, telephone or personal) and the dates of the interviews. Hence, the poll consumer must normally assume that the interview was performed competently, undoubtedly a safe assumption with reputable polling outfits. But an interviewer with the intention of generating biased responses has many opportunities in the question-asking process to achieve that end. The best way for the poll consumer to gain some sense of potential interviewer effects is to be a poll respondent who carefully observes the performance of the interviewer.

Since most citizens do not have access to raw poll data, they must rely upon the interpretations and analyses provided by the media and other sources. Therefore, the poll consumer needs to ask whether the source is likely to have a vested interest in a particular poll outcome. If so, the poll results should be scrutinized even more carefully. For example, a poll sponsored by the insurance industry purporting to demonstrate that the liability insurance crisis is due to the rapacious behavior of trial lawyers should be viewed with greater skepticism than a similar poll sponsored by an organization with a less direct interest in the outcome. Likewise, election poll results released by a candidate should be viewed more cautiously than those released by a respected news organization.

After evaluating the source of the poll, the citizen faces the more difficult task of ascertaining whether the pollster's conclusions follow from the data. This task is problematical since only a portion of the relevant evidence is often presented in a news story or press release. There may have been many items in the poll on a particular topic, yet only a subset of the items may have been reported. Of course, if one has access to the complete questionnaire, then one can tell whether only a subset of the relevant items was reported. But without knowledge of the total questionnaire, one can only hope that the analyst has reported a representative set of results or speculate how different items on the same topic might have yielded different results. Likewise, reports might include results from the entire sample, but not important variations in the responses of subsets of the sample. Lacking direct access to the data, there is little that the citizen can do about this apart from pondering how the overall results might differ within subsets of respondents.

The interpretation of a poll is not an automatic, objective enterprise; different analysts examining the same polling data may come to different conclusions. This may occur for a variety of reasons, an obvious one being that analysts may bring different values and perspectives to the interpretation of polls. Often there are no objective standards as to what constitutes a high or low level of support on an issue; it may indeed be partly cloudy or partly sunny depending upon one's perspective. Hence, the poll consumer should ask the fundamental question of whether he or she would necessarily come to the same conclusions on the basis of the data that have been presented. Just because the poll may have been sponsored by a prestigious organization and conducted by a reputable outfit does not mean that one has to defer automatically to the substantive conclusions of the sponsors. And if the poll has been conducted by an organization with an obvious vested interest in the

149

results, then independent judgments on the part of the poll consumer are certainly warranted.

Polls and the political system

Do polls promote or hinder citizens' influence in their society? Is the overall effect of the polls on the political system positive or negative? These questions continue to be vigorously debated. Writing in 1940, Cherington argued that the polls enhanced the public's influence since they provided a way for the voices of a representative cross-section of Americans to be heard; no longer would the views of a tiny segment of the population be the only ones to gain prominence. Meyer (1940) further argued that the polls provided political decision makers with accurate information about the preferences of the citizenry, thereby enabling political leaders to resist the pressures of narrow groups pushing their own special agenda in the name of the broader public.

The preceding arguments are still true today, yet the limitations inherent in polls as a mode of citizen influence must be recognized. First of all, as discussed in Chapter 1, the United States is a representative democracy that includes, in addition to elected representatives, a wide variety of organized groups trying to promote their own interests. Any assumption that the results of public opinion polls can be automatically translated into public policy is naive. Moreover, it might not be desirable if public opinion polls were routinely translated into public policy. After all, polls at times may tap only the most ephemeral and transitory of opinions. Little deliberation and thought may have gone into the responses offered by the public. And certainly the rich complexities of issues can never be captured in a public opinion poll as well as they can be in a legislative debate or a committee hearing.

Second, even if the public's views as reflected in the polls were well formed, the automatic implementation of those views might be objectionable. Often polling demonstrates that there is no majority view on an issue; opinion may be split in many different ways. The problem then becomes one of determining which subset of public opinion merits adoption. If one automatically opted for the majority or plurality position, that would call into question such cherished values as the protection of minority rights. One can envisage situations in which the unqualified use of public opinion polls might threaten rather than enhance representative democracy and related values.

Third, a focus on poll results ignores the processes by which the public's opinions are formed and modified. One factor that shapes popular opinion is the behavior of political elites. Thus, when the White House orchestrates a massive public relations campaign replete with a nationally televised presidential address, subsequent highly publicized presidential travels, and the submittal of a legislative package to the Congress, it is not surprising to see public opinion shift in the direction intended by the White House. Public opinion may not be an independent expression of the public's views, but an opinion that has been formed, at least in part, by the manipulation of elites.

For example, the president may take the lead on an issue as typically occurs during an international crisis. After a major address to the nation by the president, public opinion polls usually indicate an upsurge of support for the president's actions emerging from feelings of patriotism and a desire for national unity in times of crisis. In other cases the president may scramble to catch up with and then shape public opinion. This happened in the summer and fall of 1986 in response to Americans' heightened concern about the drug problem. With the tragic deaths of famous athletes and increased media coverage of the drug crisis, a CBS News/*New York Times* poll conducted in August 1986 showed that a plurality of Americans cited drugs as the nation's most important problem (Clymer 1986d, 1,016). The Congress, particularly House Democrats, tried to get out in front on this issue and proposed a major antidrug offensive. The White House responded by taking the initiative from Congress: the president offered his own proposals and the president and the First Lady gave an unprecedented joint address on national television. Major new legislation was passed to address the drug problem.

What do the preceding examples have to say about citizen influence? Certainly, the drug example suggests the potency of popular opinion on issues that arouse the public. But even here the salience of the drug issue was very much a function of the behavior of media and political elites who brought the issue to the fore; the public responded to the issue, but did not create it. Public attitudes can be effectively manipulated by elites to generate a desired set of opinions on an issue. In this case the adoption of drug measures into law suggests that public opinion once aroused spurs government policy initiatives. Yet even as the media and political leaders stop talking about drugs, the issue may recede from popular consciousness, and citizens may have a misguided feeling that somehow the problem has been resolved.

The international crisis example raises a different problem—namely, elites' misinterpretation (deliberate or unintentional) of what the polls are actually saying. Unfortunately, political leaders sometimes fail to recognize the limitations and circumstances of poll responses and automatically construe supportive poll results as ringing endorsements of a broad policy agenda. The tendency of Americans to rally around the opinion leadership of the president during an international crisis should not be blindly interpreted as a popular mandate for particular policies.

Ginsberg (1986) has argued that polling weakens the influence of public opinion in a democratic society. He aserts that there are many ways besides participating in a poll for citizens to express their opinions, such as demonstrations and protests, letter-writing campaigns, and interest group activities. But because polling is deemed to be scientific and representative of the broad public, it has dominated these other types of expression.

Ginsberg identifies four basic changes in the nature of public opinion that are attributable to the rise of polling. First, responding to a public opinion survey is an easier form of expression than writing a letter or participating in a protest—activities usually performed by citizens who are intensely committed to their positions. But anyone of any opinion intensity can respond to a poll question. Hence, in a public opinion poll the intense opinions of a small minority may be submerged by the indifferent views of the sizable majority. Indeed, government leaders may try to dismiss the views of dissidents by citing polls that indicate that most Americans do not support their position.

Second, polling changes public opinion from a *behavior*, such as letter writing or demonstrating, to an *attitude*, as revealed in a verbal response to a poll question. Ginsberg argues that public opinion expressed through polls is less threatening to political elites than are opinions expressed through behavioral mechanisms. Moreover, polls can inform leaders about dissidents' attitudes before they become behaviors, thereby giving government a form of early warning and the opportunity to change attitudes by actually remedying problems or by relying on public relations techniques to manipulate opinions.

Third, polls convert public opinion from being a characteristic of groups to being an attribute of individuals. This enables public officials to ignore group leaders and attend instead to the opinions of citizens directly. Unfortunately, this may effectively weaken individuals' political power since organized activity, not individual activity, is the key to citizen influence in the United States. If government leaders are able to use the polls as an excuse to ignore group preferences, then citizen influence will be lessened.

Finally, polling reduces citizens' opportunities to set the political agenda. The topics of public opinion polls are those selected by the polls' sponsors rather than by the citizenry. Therefore, citizens lose control over the issue agenda, and the agenda as revealed through the polls may differ in major ways from the issues that are truly important to people.

Ginsberg's fundamental conclusion is that polling makes public opinion safer and less threatening for government. Opinions expressed through the polls place fewer demands and constraints on decision makers and provide political leaders with an enhanced ability "to anticipate, regulate, and manipulate popular attitudes" (Ginsberg 1986, 85). In short, Ginsberg's thesis is that the advent and growth of public opinion polling have been a detriment to citizen influence.

Observers have been concerned about the effect of polls not only on citizens' political clout but also on the performance of elected office-holders. Over forty years ago Bernays (1945) warned that the polls would dominate the political leadership, that decision makers would slavishly follow the polls in order to please the people and maintain their popularity. The polls might even paralyze political leaders, preventing them from taking unpopular positions and from trying to educate the public on controversial issues. Political observers still contemptuously deride politicians who run around with polls in their pockets, lacking the courage of their own convictions no matter what the polls say.

Although some officeholders blindly follow the polls, today the greater concern is over those who use, abuse, manipulate, and misinterpret them. In particular, presidents have increasingly tried to manage and manipulate public opinion. For example, Altschuler (1986) describes how Lyndon Johnson tried to take the offensive when his poll ratings started to decline. To convince key elites that he was still strong, Johnson attacked the public polls, selectively leaked private polls, and tried to influence poll results and poll reporting by cultivating the pollsters.

The Reagan presidency has developed one of the most skillful public relations efforts; in-house polling is a central part of the enterprise (Blumenthal 1981). Writing about the Reagan administration, Beal and Hinckley (1984) argued that polls became more important after the presidential election than before it, that polls were a much more important tool of governing than was commonly recognized. Certainly, no one would deny the president and other elected officials their pollsters. But the measure of an incumbent's performance should not simply be the degree of success achieved in shaping public opinion in particular ways.

One final effect of polls on the political system merits consideration—namely, the contribution of polls to political discourse. As topics of conversation, the polls contribute to political debate. The polls are often cited as evidence in support of particular positions and as such become a central part of political discussion. But polls have more subtle effects; in particular, Americans' awareness of the attitudes of their fellow citizens as learned through the polls may alter their opinions and subsequent behaviors. This phenomenon has been explained in terms of the theories of pluralistic ignorance and the spiral of silence.

The spiral of silence thesis, developed by Noelle-Neuman (1974, 1977), argues that individuals desire to be respected and popular. To accomplish this, they are very sensitive to the prevailing opinions and how they are changing. If individuals observe that their opinions seem to be in the minority and are losing support, they are less likely to express them publicly. Consequently, such opinions will appear to be weaker than they actually are. On the other hand, if people perceive that their views are popular and on the ascendance, they are more likely to discuss them openly. Such opinions then gain more adherents and seem stronger than they actually are. Hence, one opinion gets established as the dominant one, while the other recedes to the background. Pluralistic ignorance (O'Gorman 1975; O'Gorman and Garry 1976-1977) refers to people's misperception of what other individuals and groups believe. This, in turn, affects their own views and their willingness to express them.

Lang and Lang (1984) thus link the notions of pluralistic ignorance and the spiral of silence in a discussion of American racial attitudes:

> Typical of pluralistic ignorance has been the unwillingness of many whites to acknowledge their own antiblack prejudice, which they believe to contradict an accepted cultural ideal. As a way of justifying their own behavior, these whites often attribute such prejudice to other whites by saying "I wouldn't mind having a black neighbor except that my neighbors wouldn't stand for it."
> But what if such fears about their neighbors' reactions proved unjustified? What if polls showed an expressed readiness for a range of desegregation measures that these whites do not believe others are prepared to accept? Such a finding contrary to prevailing belief would be controversial. Where the real opinion lies may be less important than the change in perception of the climate of opinion. A definitive poll finding can destroy the premise that underlies the justification for behavior clearly at variance with professed ideals. In these circumstances a spiral of silence about the real opinion fosters a climate inhospitable to segregationist sentiment and drives it underground. (Lang and Lang 1984, 141)

PEANUTS 10-11-86-© United Features Syndicate, Inc.

As this example illustrates, public opinion polls provide us with a mechanism for knowing what our fellow citizens think and believe. If the polls can accurately measure the underlying beliefs and values of the citizenry, then we no longer have to be at the mercy of unrepresentative views that mistakenly are thought of as the majority voice. The polls can tell us a lot about ourselves as part of American society, and this self-knowledge may foster a healthier and more open political debate.

Conclusion

As the Peanuts cartoon makes clear, Americans have ambivalent feelings about the polls. We resent the polls when they become too intrusive and seem to be telling us what we will be doing even before we do it. Yet we are also fascinated by what the polls tell us about ourselves. We are suspicious because we seldom if ever are respondents in a poll, yet we readily cite the surveys conducted by reputable and even disreputable pollsters. We complain about the pervasiveness of polls, yet are apt to raise questions that can be answered only by polls.

Perhaps this ambivalence arises out of our uncertainty about just what goes into a poll. Polls are called scientific, yet we know that they are sometimes wrong. Politicians one day swear by the polls, while the next day they swear at them. We would be in a better position to evaluate the polls if we understood those factors that can affect poll results. Thus, the aim of this book has been to remove the mystery of public opinion research and in this way help the consumer come to terms with the polls. Only then can the citizen master the polls rather than be mastered by them.

References

Abrams, Floyd. 1985. "Press Practices, Polling Restrictions, Public Opinion and First Amendment Guarantees." *Public Opinion Quarterly*, vol. 49, no. 1 (Spring): 15-18.

Aldrich, John H., et al. 1982. "The Measurement of Public Opinion about Public Policy: A Report on Some New Issue Question Formats." *American Journal of Political Science*, vol. 26, no. 2 (May): 391-414.

Alpern, David M. 1986. A *Newsweek* Poll: Sex Laws." *Newsweek*, 14 July, 38.

Altschuler, Bruce E. 1986. "Lyndon Johnson and the Public Polls." *Public Opinion Quarterly*, vol. 50, no. 3 (Fall): 285-299.

Anderson, Barbara A., Brian D. Silver, and Paul R. Abramson. 1986. "The Effects of Race of Interviewers in SRC National Election Studies." Paper presented at the annual meeting of the American Political Science Association, Washington, D.C., 28-31 August.

Apple, R. W., Jr. 1986. "President Highly Popular in Poll; No Ideological Shift is Discerned." *New York Times*, 28 January, A-1, A-14.

Asher, Herbert B. 1974a. "The Reliability of the Political Efficacy Items." *Political Methodology*, vol. 1, no. 2 (May): 45-72.

_____. 1974b. "Some Consequences of Measurement Error in Survey Data." *American Journal of Political Science*, vol. 18, no. 2 (May): 469-485.

_____. 1974c. "Some Problems in the Use of Multiple Indicators." Paper presented at a Conference on Design and Measurement Standards for Research in Political Science, Delevan, Wis., 13-15 May.

_____. 1984. *Presidential Elections and American Politics*. 3d ed. Homewood, Ill.: The Dorsey Press.

Baron, Alan. 1980. "The Slippery Art of Polls." *Politics Today*, vol. 7, no. 1 (January/February): 21-24.

Beal, Richard S., and Ronald H. Hinckley. 1984. "Presidential Decision Making and Opinion Polls." *The Annals of the American Academy of Political and Social Science*, vol. 472 (March): 72-84.

Bernays, Edward L. 1945. "Attitude Polls—Servants or Masters?" *Public Opinion Quarterly*, vol. 9, no. 3 (Fall): 264-268b.

Bishop. George F., Robert W. Oldendick, and Alfred J. Tuchfarber. 1982. "Political Information Processing: Question Order and Context Effects."

157

Political Behavior, vol. 4, no. 2, 177-200.

_____. 1984. "What Must My Interest in Politics Be If I Just Told You 'I Don't Know'?" *Public Opinion Quarterly*, vol. 48, no. 2 (Summer): 510-519.

Bishop, George F., et al. 1980. "Pseudo-Opinions on Public Affairs." *Public Opinion Quarterly*, vol. 44, no. 2 (Summer): 198-209.

Blumenthal, Sidney. 1981. "Marketing the President." *New York Times Magazine*, 13 September, 43, 110-118.

Broder, David S. 1982. "Daily Polls Helped GOP Keep Senate Edge." *Washington Post*, 7 November, 1.

_____. 1984. "The Needless Exit-Polls Battle." *Washington Post*, national weekly ed., 2 January, 4.

Broh, C. Anthony. 1980. "Horse-Race Journalism: Reporting the Polls in the 1976 Presidential Election." *Public Opinion Quarterly*, vol. 44, no. 4 (Winter): 514-529.

Brown, Phil. 1982. "Attitudes Towards the Rights of Mental Patients—A National Survey in the United States." *Social Science and Medicine*, vol. 16, no. 23, 2025-2039.

Busch, Ronald J., and Joel A. Lieske. 1985. "Does Time of Voting Affect Exit Poll Results?" *Public Opinion Quarterly*, vol. 49, no. 1 (Spring): 94-104.

Campbell, Bruce A. 1981. "Race-of-Interviewer Effects among Southern Adolescents." *Public Opinion Quarterly*, vol. 45, no. 2 (Summer): 231-244.

Cherington, Paul T. 1940. "Opinion Polls as the Voice of Democracy." *Public Opinion Quarterly*, vol. 4, no. 2 (June): 236-238.

Clymer, Adam. 1985. "Pollsters Cite Surveys Indicating Confidence in their Work." *New York Times*, 20 May, B-7.

_____. 1986a. "Most Blacks Back Reagan, Poll Finds." *New York Times*, 5 January, 20.

_____. 1986b. "One Issue That Seems To Defy a Yes or No." *New York Times*, 23 February, 22-E.

_____. 1986c. "A Poll Finds 77% in U.S. Approve Raid on Libya." *New York Times*, 17 April, A-23.

_____. 1986d. "Public Found Ready to Sacrifice in Drug Fight. *New York Times*, 2 September, 1, D-16.

Converse, Jean M. 1976-1977. "Predicting No Opinion in the Polls." *Public Opinion Quarterly*, vol. 40, no. 4 (Winter): 515-530.

Converse, Philip E. 1970. "Attitudes and Nonattitudes: Continuation of a Dialogue." In *The Quantitative Analysis of Social Problems*, ed. Edward Tufte, 168-189. Reading, Mass.: Addison-Wesley.

Coombs, Clyde H., and Lolagene C. Coombs. 1976-1977. " 'Don't Know': Item Ambiguity or Respondent Uncertainty?" *Public Opinion Quarterly*, vol. 40, no. 4 (Winter): 497-514.

Cotter, Patrick R., Jeffrey Cohen, and Philip B. Coulter. 1982. "Race-of-Interviewer Effects on Telephone Interviews." *Public Opinion Quarterly*, vol. 46, no. 2 (Summer): 278-284.

Crespi, Irving. 1980. "Polls as Journalism." *Public Opinion Quarterly*, vol. 44, no. 4 (Winter): 462-476.

Crossley, Archibald M., and Helen M. Crossley. 1969. "Polling in 1968." *Public Opinion Quarterly*, vol. 33, no. 1 (Spring): 1-16.

Curtin, Michael. 1986a. "Celeste Leading Rhodes 48% to 43%, with Kucinich

Trailing." *Columbus Dispatch,* 10 August, 1-A.

_____. 1986b. "Here Is How Poll Was Taken." *Columbus Dispatch,* 10 August, 8-E.

Day, Richard, and Kurt M. Becker. 1984. "Preelection Polling in the 1982 Illinois Gubernatorial Contest." *Public Opinion Quarterly,* vol. 48, no. 3 (Fall): 606-614.

de Bock, Harold. 1976. "Influence of In-State Election Poll Reports on Candidate Preference in 1972." *Journalism Quarterly,* vol. 53, no. 3 (Autumn): 457-462.

DeClercq, Eugene R. 1983. "Public Opinion Toward Midwifery and Home Birth: An Exploratory Analysis." *Journal of Nurse-Midwifery,* vol. 28, no. 3 (May/June): 19-21.

Delli Carpini, Michael X. 1984. "Scooping the Voters? The Consequences of the Networks' Early Call of the 1980 Presidential Race." *The Journal of Politics,* vol. 46, no. 3 (August): 866-885.

Dionne, E. J., Jr. 1980. "The Debate Decision Put Polls and Pollsters on the Firing Line." *New York Times,* 14 September, E-3.

Dolnick, Edward. 1984. "Pollsters Are Asking: What's Wrong." *Columbus Dispatch,* 19 August, C-1.

Dutka, Solomon. 1982. "Bringing Polls to Justice." *Public Opinion,* vol. 5, no. 5 (October/November): 47-49.

Epstein, Laurily, and Gerald Strom. 1984. "Survey Research and Election Night Projections." *Public Opinion,* vol. 7, no. 1 (February/March): 48-50.

Erikson, Robert S. 1976. "The Relationship between Public Opinion and State Policy: A New Look Based on Some Forgotten Data." *American Journal of Political Science,* vol. 20, no. 1 (February): 25-36.

Eubank, Robert B., and David John Gow. 1983. "The Pro-Incumbent Bias in the 1978 and 1980 National Election Studies." *American Journal on Political Science,* vol. 27, no. 1 (February): 122-139.

Faulkenberry, G. David, and Robert Mason. 1978. "Characteristics of Nonopinion and No Opinion Response Groups." *Public Opinion Quarterly,* vol. 42, no. 4 (Winter): 533-543.

Felson, Marcus, and Seymour Sudman. 1975. "The Accuracy of Presidential-Preference Primary Polls." *Public Opinion Quarterly,* vol. 39, no. 2 (Summer): 232-236.

Frey, James H. 1983. *Survey Research by Telephone.* Beverly Hills: Sage Publications.

Gallup, George. 1947. "The Quintamensional Plan of Question Design." *Public Opinion Quarterly,* vol. 11, no. 3 (Fall): 385-393.

_____. 1965-1966. "Polls and the Political Process—Past, Present, and Future." *Public Opinion Quarterly,* vol. 29, no. 4 (Winter): 544-549.

Galtung, Johan. 1969. *Theory and Methods of Social Research.* New York: Columbia University Press.

Ginsberg, Benjamin. 1986. *The Captive Public: How Mass Opinion Promotes State Power.* New York: Basic Books.

Goldhaber, Gerald M. 1984. "A Pollster's Sampler." *Public Opinion,* vol. 7, no. 3 (June/July): 47-50, 53.

Gow, David John, and Robert B. Eubank. 1984. "The Pro-Incumbent Bias in the 1982 National Election Study." *American Journal of Political Science,* vol. 27, no. 1 (February): 224-230.

Goyder, John. 1985. "Face-to-Face Interviews and Mailed Questionnaires: The Net Difference in Response Rate." *Public Opinion Quarterly,* vol. 49, no. 2

159

(Summer): 234-252.

Greenberg, Daniel S. 1980. "The Plague of Polling." *Washington Post*, 16 September, A-17.

Grodsky, Phyllis B. 1983. "Public Opinion on Animal-based Research—The Unknown Factor in Ethical and Policy Decisions." *Annals of the New York Academy of Sciences*, vol. 406, 20 June, 157-158.

Hatchett, S., and H. Schuman. 1975-1976. "White Respondents and Race-of-Interviewer Effects." *Public Opinion Quarterly*, vol. 39, no. 4 (Winter): 523-528.

Herbers, John. 1982. "Polls Find Conflict in Views on Aid and Public Welfare." *New York Times*, 14 February, 19.

Hyman, Herbert H., and Paul B. Sheatsley. 1950. "The Current Status of American Public Opinion." In *The Teaching of Contemporary Affairs*, ed. J. C. Payne, 11-34. Twenty-first Yearbook of the National Council of Social Studies.

Jackson, John. 1983. "Election Night Reporting and Voter Turnout." *American Journal of Political Science*, vol. 27, no. 4 (November): 615-635.

Jackson, John, and William McGee. 1981. "Election Reporting and Voter Turnout." Report of the Center for Political Studies, the University of Michigan, Ann Arbor.

Jordan, Gene. 1982. "Polls Reflect Participants' Mood at Time Taken." *Columbus Dispatch*, 16 May, C-1.

Keene, Karlyn H., and Victoria A. Sackett. 1981. "An Editors' Report on the Yankelovich, Skelly and White 'Mushiness Index,'" *Public Opinion*, vol. 4, no. 2 (April/May): 50-51.

Kinder, Donald R., and Lynn M. Sanders. 1986. "Survey Questions and Political Culture: The Case of Whites' Response to Affirmative Action for Blacks." Paper presented at the annual meeting of the American Political Science Association, Washington, D.C., 28-31 August.

Knap, Ted. 1980. "League Weighs Anderson's Standing for Debates." *Columbus Citizen-Journal*, 9 September, 7.

Koch, Nadine S. 1985. *Perceptions of Public Opinion Polls*. Ph.D. diss., Ohio State University.

Kohut, Andrew. 1983. "Illinois Politics Confound the Polls." *Public Opinion*, vol. 5, no. 6 (December/January): 42-43.

Kostrzewa, John. 1986a. "Celeste Holds Early Lead in Race." *Akron Beacon Journal*, 23 March, A-1.

———. 1986b. "Rhodes Has Solid Edge over Primary Rivals." *Akron Beacon Journal*, 23 March, A-5.

Ladd, Everett Carll. 1980. "Polling and the Press: The Clash of Institutional Imperatives." *Public Opinion Quarterly*, vol. 44, no. 4 (Winter): 574-584.

Lang, Kurt, and Gladys Engel Lang. 1984. "The Impact of Polls on Public Opinion." *The Annals of the American Academy of Political and Social Science*, vol. 472 (March): 130-142.

Lardner, George, Jr. 1985. "A Majority of the People Are against the 'Star Wars' Defense Plan." *Washington Post*, national weekly ed., 9 September, 37.

Lavrakas, Paul J. 1986. "Surveying the Survey Differences." *Chicago Tribune*, 17 June, 12.

Lelyveld, Joseph. 1986. "Britain Heads for Nuclear War at Polls." *New York Times*, 5 October, 2-E.

Levy, Mark R. 1983. "The Methodology and Performance of Election Day Polls." *Public Opinion Quarterly*, vol. 47, no. 1 (Spring): 54-67.

Lewis, I. A., and William Schneider. 1982. "Is the Public Lying to the Pollsters?" *Public Opinion*, vol. 5, no. 2 (April/May): 42-47.

Lichter, Linda S. 1985. "Who Speaks for Black America?" *Public Opinion*, vol. 8, no. 4 (August/September): 41-44, 58.

Lipset, Seymour Martin. 1980. "Different Polls, Different Results in 1980 Politics." *Public Opinion*, vol. 3, no. 4 (August/September): 19-20, 60.

Margolis, Michael. 1984. "Public Opinion, Polling, and Political Behavior." *The Annals of the American Academy of Political and Social Science*, vol. 472 (March): 61-71.

Marks, Amy Seidel, and Bobby J. Calder. 1982. *Attitudes Toward Death and Funerals*. Evanston, Ill.: Center for Marketing Sciences, J. L. Kellogg Graduate School of Management.

Marsh, Catherine. 1984. "Do Polls Affect What People Think?" In *Surveying Subjective Phenomena*, ed. Charles F. Turner and Elizabeth Martin, vol. 2, 565-591. New York: Russell Sage Foundation.

Meislin, Richard J. 1987. "Racial Divisions Seen in Poll on Howard Beach Attack." *New York Times*, 8 January, 16.

Meyer, Eugene. 1940. "A Newspaper Publisher Looks at the Polls." *Public Opinion Quarterly*, vol. 4, no. 2 (June): 238-240.

Miller, M. Mark, and Robert Hurd. 1982. "Conformity to AAPOR Standards in Newspaper Reporting of Public Opinion Polls." *Public Opinion Quarterly*, vol. 46, no. 2 (Summer): 243-249.

Miller, Tim. 1986. "Statewide Poll Has Rhodes Far Ahead in GOP." *Dayton Daily News*, 23 March, 1.

Mitofsky, Warren J., and Martin Plissner. 1980. "A Reporter's Guide to Published Polls." *Public Opinion*, vol. 3, no. 3 (June/July): 16-19.

Morganthau, Tom. 1986. "Four More Years?" *Newsweek*, 8 September, 16-17.

Morrison, Perry R. 1983. "A Survey of Attitudes Toward Computers." *Communications of the ACM*, vol. 26, no. 12 (December): 1051-1057.

Neevel, Jeanne. 1982. *A Survey of Attitudes of Males Toward Menopause*. M.S. thesis, University of Oregon.

Neuman, W. Russell. 1986. *The Paradox of Mass Politics: Knowledge and Opinion in the American Electorate*. Cambridge, Mass.: Harvard University Press.

Newman, Jody. 1983. "Taking on an Incumbent: The Remarkable Woods-Danforth 1982 U.S. Senate Race." *Campaigns and Elections*, vol. 4, no. 1 (Spring): 29-39.

Nietzel, Michael T., and Ronald C. Dillehay. 1983. "Psychologists as Consultants for Changes of Venue: The Use of Public Opinion Surveys." *Law and Human Behavior*, vol. 7, no. 4 (December): 309-335.

Noelle-Neumann, Elisabeth. 1974. "The Spiral of Silence: A Theory of Public Opinion." *Journal of Communication*, vol. 24, no. 2 (Spring): 43-51.

_____. 1977. "Turbulence in the Climate of Opinion: Methodological Applications of the Spiral of Silence Theory." *Public Opinion Quarterly*, vol. 41, no. 2 (Summer): 143-158.

Norpoth, Helmut, and Milton Lodge. 1985. "The Difference between Attitudes and Nonattitudes in the Mass Public: Just Measurement?" *American Journal of Political Science*, vol. 29, no. 2 (May): 291-307.

O'Gorman, Hubert J. 1975. "Pluralistic Ignorance and White Estimates of White Support for Racial Segregation." *Public Opinion Quarterly*, vol. 39, no. 3 (Fall): 313-330.

O'Gorman, Hubert J., and Stephen L. Garry. 1976-1977. "Pluralistic Ignorance— A Replication and Extension." *Public Opinion Quarterly*, vol. 40, no. 4 (Winter): 449-458.

Oreskes, Michael. 1984. "Pollsters Offer Reasons for Disparity in Results." *New York Times*, 20 October, A-8.

Orton, Barry. 1982. "Phony Polls: The Pollster's Nemesis." *Public Opinion*, vol. 5, no. 3 (June/July): 56-60.

Page, Benjamin I., and Robert Y. Shapiro. 1983. "Effects of Public Opinion on Policy." *American Political Science Review*, vol. 77, no. 1 (March): 175-190.

Paletz, David L., et. al. 1980. "Polls in the Media: Content, Credibility, and Consequences." *Public Opinion Quarterly*, vol. 44, no. 4 (Winter): 495-513.

Payne, Stanley L. 1951. *The Art of Asking Questions*. Princeton, N.J.: Princeton University Press.

Perry, Paul. 1979. "Certain Problems in Election Survey Methodology." *Public Opinion Quarterly*, vol. 43, no. 3 (Fall): 312-325.

Peterson, Robert A. 1984. "Asking the Age Question: A Research Note." *Public Opinion Quarterly*, vol. 48, no. 1-B (Spring): 379-383.

Phillips, Kevin P. 1976. "Polls Used to Reflect Electability." *Columbus Dispatch*, 19 July, B-2.

———. 1981. "Polls Are Too Broad in Analysis Divisions." *Columbus Dispatch*, 8 September B-3.

Presser, Stanley, and Howard Schuman. 1980. "The Measurement of a Middle Position in Attitude Surveys." *Public Opinion Quarterly*, vol. 44, no. 1 (Spring): 70-85.

Raines, Howell. 1984. "Talking Points: Debates Shift the Focus and Perhaps the Odds." *New York Times*, 14 October, 1-E.

Reading, Anthony E., Caroline M. Sledmere, and David N. Cox. 1982. "A Survey of Patient Attitudes towards Artificial Insemination by Donor." *Journal of Psychosomatic Research*, vol. 26, no. 4, 429-433.

Reese, Stephen D., et al. 1986. "Ethnicity-of-Interviewer Effects among Mexican-Americans and Anglos." *Public Opinion Quarterly*, vol. 50, no. 4 (Winter): 563-572.

Robbins, William. 1986. "Surge in Sympathy for Farmer Found." *New York Times*, 25 February, A-1.

Robinson, Michael J., and Margaret A. Sheehan. 1983. *Over the Wire and on TV: CBS and UPI in Campaign '80*. New York: Russell Sage Foundation.

Roper, Burns W. 1985. "Early Election Calls: The Larger Dangers." *Public Opinion Quarterly*, vol. 49, no. 1 (Spring): 5-9.

Rothenberg, Stuart, ed. 1982. *The Political Report*, vol. 5, no. 42, 27 October.

———. 1983. *The Political Report*, vol. 6, no. 31, 5 August.

———. 1985. *The Political Report*, vol. 8, no. 43, 25 October.

———. 1986a. *The Political Report*, vol. 9, no. 28, 11 July.

———. 1986b. *The Political Report*, vol. 9, no. 30, 25 July.

———. 1986c. *The Political Report*, vol. 9, no. 37, 12 September.

Salwen, Michael B. 1985a. "Does Poll Coverage Improve as Presidential Vote Nears?" *Journalism Quarterly*, vol. 62, no. 4 (Winter): 887-891.

_____. 1985b. "The Reporting of Public Opinion Polls During Presidential Years, 1968-1984." *Journalism Quarterly*, vol. 62, no. 2 (Summer): 272-277.

Schuman, Howard, Graham Kalton, and Jacob Ludwig. 1983. "Context and Contiguity in Survey Questionnaires." *Public Opinion Quarterly*, vol. 47, no. 1 (Spring): 112-115.

Schuman, Howard, and Jean M. Converse. 1971. "The Effects of Black and White Interviewers on Black Responses in 1968." *Public Opinion Quarterly*, vol. 35, no. 1 (Spring): 44-68.

Schuman, Howard, and Stanley Presser. 1977. "Question Wording as an Independent Variable in Survey Analysis." *Sociological Methods and Research*, vol. 6, no. 2 (November): 151-170.

_____. 1980. "Public Opinion and Public Ignorance: The Fine Line between Attitudes and Nonattitudes." *American Journal of Sociology*, vol. 85, no. 5 (March): 1214-1225.

_____. 1981. *Questions and Answers in Attitude Surveys: Experiments on Question Form, Wording, and Context.* New York: Academic Press.

Schuman, Howard, Stanley Presser, and Jacob Ludwig. 1981. "Context Effects on Survey Responses to Questions about Abortion." *Public Opinion Quarterly*, vol. 45, no. 2 (Summer): 216-223.

Shipler, David K. 1986. "Public Is Confused on Contra Aid Issue, Poll Indicates." *New York Times*, 15 April, 4.

Sigelman, Lee. 1981. "Question-Order Effects on Presidential Popularity." *Public Opinion Quarterly*, vol. 45, no. 2 (Summer): 199-207.

Sigelman, Lee, and Carol K. Sigelman. 1984. "Judgments of the Carter-Reagan Debate: The Eyes of the Beholders." *Public Opinion Quarterly*, vol. 48, no. 3 (Fall): 624-628.

Slater, Dan, and Valerie P. Hans. 1984. "Public Opinion of Forensic Psychiatry Following the Hinckley Verdict." *American Journal of Psychiatry*, vol. 141, no. 5 (May): 675-679.

Smith, Ted J., III, and Derek O. Verrall. 1985. "A Critical Analysis of Australian Television Coverage of Election Opinion Polls." *Public Opinion Quarterly*, vol. 49, no. 1 (Spring): 58-79.

Smith, Tom W. 1984. "Nonattitudes: A Review and Evaluation." In *Surveying Subjective Phenomena*, ed. Charles F. Turner and Elizabeth Martin, vol. 2, 215-255. New York: Russell Sage Foundation.

Steeh, Charlotte G. 1981. "Trends in Nonresponse Rates, 1952-1979." *Public Opinion Quarterly*, vol. 45, no. 1 (Spring): 40-57.

Stinchcombe, Arthur L., Calvin Jones, and Paul Sheatsley. 1981. "Nonresponse Bias for Attitude Questions." *Public Opinion Quarterly*, vol. 45, no. 3 (Fall): 359-375.

Sudman, Seymour. 1986. "Do Exit Polls Influence Voting Behavior?" *Public Opinion Quarterly*, vol. 50, no. 3 (Fall): 331-339.

Sussman, Barry. 1984a. "Why Both Parties Are Courting 50 Million Opinion-Switchers." *Washington Post*, national weekly ed., 16 January, 37.

_____. 1984b. "Already the Polls Are Getting Difficult to Follow." *Washington Post*, 26 January, A-2.

_____. 1984c. "Do-It-Yourself Tax Reform: Many Think Cheating Is Okay." *Washington Post*, national weekly ed., 28 May, 36.

_____. 1984d. "Some Answers to the Polls' Critics." *Washington Post*, national

163

weekly ed., 12 November, 37.

———. 1985a. "To Understand These Polls, You Have to Read the Fine Print." *Washington Post,* national weekly ed., 4 March, 37.

———. 1985b. "Reagan's Support on Issues Relies Heavily on the Uninformed." *Washington Post,* national weekly ed., 1 April, 37.

———. 1985c. "Americans Prefer Tax Cheating to Being Paid to Inform the IRS." *Washington Post,* national weekly ed., 13 May, 37.

———. 1985d. "Social Security and the Young." *Washington Post,* national weekly ed., 27 May, 37.

———. 1985e. "Pollsters Cheer up about Public's Opinions of Polls." *Washington Post,* national weekly ed., 3 June, 37.

———. 1985f. "Do Pre-Election Polls Influence People to Switch Their Votes?" *Washington Post,* national weekly ed., 10 June, 37.

———. 1985g. "Loaded Questions, Faulty Data." *Washington Post,* national weekly ed., 14 October, 37.

———. 1985h. "These Polls Are Part Public Opinion, Part Public Relations." *Washington Post,* national weekly ed., 4 November, 37.

———. 1985i. "On 'Star Wars,' It All Depends on How You Ask the Question." *Washington Post,* national weekly ed., 25 November, 37.

———. 1986a. "Do Blacks Approve of Reagan? It Depends on Who's Asking." *Washington Post,* national weekly ed., 10 February, 37.

———. 1986b. "It's Wrong to Assume that School Busing Is Wildly Unpopular." *Washington Post,* national weekly ed., 10 March, 37.

———. 1986c. "With Pornography, It All Depends on Who's Doing the Looking." *Washington Post,* national weekly ed., 24 March, 37.

———. 1986d. "Right Now Hart Would Beat Bush." *Washington Post,* national weekly ed., 9 June, 14.

Swift, Al. 1985. "The Congressional Concern about Early Calls." *Public Opinion Quarterly,* vol. 49, no. 1 (Spring): 2-5.

Taylor, Marylee C. 1983. "The Black-and-White Model of Attitude Stability: A Latent Class Examination of Opinion and Nonopinion in the American Public." *American Journal of Sociology,* vol. 89, no. 2 (September): 373-401.

Townley, Rod. 1980. "TV's Campaign Polls: How Much Can We Believe?" *TV Guide,* 6 September, 23-26.

Weeks, Michael F., and R. Paul Moore. 1981. "Ethnicity-of-Interviewer Effects on Ethnic Respondents." *Public Opinion Quarterly,* vol. 45, no. 2 (Summer): 245-249.

Wilcox, William Clyde. 1984. *The New Christian Right and the White Fundamentalists: An Analysis of a Potential Political Movement.* Ph.D. diss., Ohio State University.

Williams, Dennis A. 1979. "A New Racial Poll." *Newsweek,* 26 February, 48, 53.

Williams, Juan. 1985. "Poll Irks Black Leaders." *Washington Post,* 30 September, A-11.

Wright, James D. 1981. "Public Opinion and Gun Control: A Comparison of Results from Two Recent National Surveys." *The Annals of the American Academy of Political and Social Science,* vol. 455 (May): 24-39.

Index ━━━━━━━━━━━━━━━━━━━━━━━━━━━━━

165

Index

Index